Contents

Trouble-shooting

Yo

A step-by

Geof

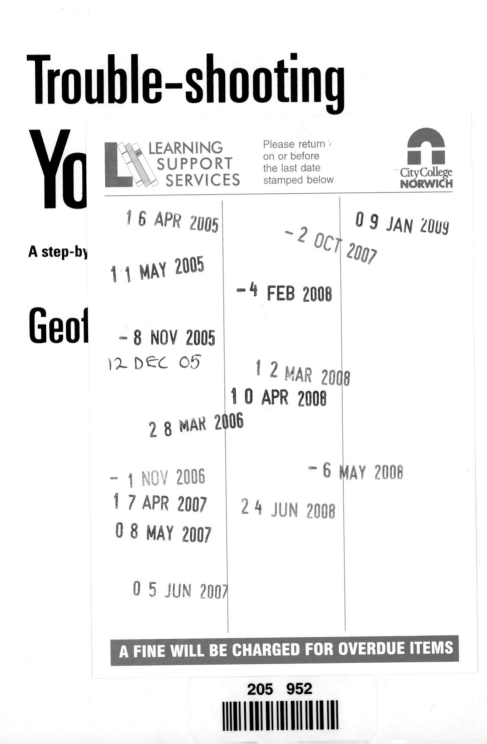

First published in Great Britain and the United States in 2003 by Kogan Page Limited

Reprinted 2004 by RoutledgeFalmer
11 New Fetter Lane
London EC4P 4EE

RoutledgeFalmer is an imprint of the Taylor & Francis Group

ISBN 0 7494 3775 8

British Library Cataloguing in Publication Data

A CIP record for this book is available from the British Library.

Library of Congress Cataloguing in Publication Data

Squires, Geoffrey.
  Trouble-shooting your teaching : a step-by-step guide to analysing and improving your practice / Geoffrey Squires.
        p. cm.
Includes bibliographical references (p. 199)
    ISBN 0-7494-3775-8
  1. Effective teaching. 2. Teaching–Evaluation. I. Title.
    LB1025.3 .S693 2003
    371.102–dc21

                                                                        2002013429

Typeset by JS Typesetting Ltd, Wellingborough, Northants.
Printed and bound in Great Britain by Biddles Ltd, King's Lynn, Norfolk

Acknowledgements

I would like to record my thanks to the University of Hull for a grant that enabled me to complete the work on this book and to those colleagues both in the University and in schools and colleges in the Yorkshire region who kindly commented on an earlier draft. I have incorporated many of their suggestions in the final text. I am also grateful to Jonathan Simpson at Kogan Page for his guidance, help and support at every stage in the project.

Introduction

The aim of this book is to help you identify any aspects of your teaching that are not working as well as they might and to do something about them.

The book is geared primarily to those who teach in the post-compulsory field, whether in schools or colleges, further or higher education, or in the various forms of adult, continuing education. Much of it is relevant to teaching students of 14+ as well, although if you work with this age group you may need to adapt some of it in your own mind in order to relate what is said to your situation. Because of the growing overlap between education and training, there are some references to the latter as well.

Trouble-shooting in teaching is not as straightforward or neat a matter as it is in a technical setting. We are not talking about car engines or software systems here, but about a human activity with all the subtleties and differences of experience and perception that this brings. However, technical repair work is still a useful metaphor because it implies the need to pinpoint or pin down the source of a problem in what is a complex, interactive whole. Often in teaching – as elsewhere – we get the sense that things are not going as well as they should, but find it difficult to identify the precise locus or cause of the problem. Teaching is a many-faceted activity, involving not only the interplay of structures, resources and activities within a prescribed time frame, but a wide range of actors or players: students, teachers, managers and support staff, not to mention external stakeholders such as parents, employers, communities, public agencies and ultimately government. Faced with that heaving mass of complexity, we can find it hard to know where to look for the origin of problems.

This book should help you to do just that. It takes you step by step through a series of diagnostic questions, related first to the class or session, then to the course or programme, and finally to the wider management of teaching. In many cases, you will be able to give a positive answer to the initial question and move on, although even then it may be useful to scan through the text for relevant points or new ideas. However, every so often a question will ring a bell or set lights flashing (to continue the technical metaphor). You may find that some of the issues are related and that there is, in fact, a cluster of problems, each of which impacts on and perhaps exacerbates the others. You may come to realize that the main problems lie at one of the three main levels of analysis: session, course or management. If so, that is an important finding because it directs your attention and energies towards certain kinds of changes, while leaving other things alone; and it is important that we do leave well alone, because constant tinkering and change undermine the routines and expectations that both teachers and learners need to build up.

This general introduction explains how to use the book. You can work through it either on your own or with a group of colleagues, though normally you will get more out of the second approach because different people will bring different perspectives to what is going on. You can dip into it or read it right through. You can use the book repeatedly, since problems change over time. It also forms a resource for organized staff development events, either within or across institutions; indeed, a variety of settings can throw up interesting contrasts and comparisons.

Post-compulsory education is a remarkably diverse field. One aspect of this is the variety of staff labels: teacher, lecturer, tutor, supervisor, facilitator, instructor, trainer. Here, everyone is referred to simply as a *teacher*, regardless of formal title, because that is what he or she does, and likewise the learners – of all kinds – are referred to as *students*. Similarly, schools, colleges, universities, centres and services are all described as *institutions*. However, feel free to substitute your own terms if they are more familiar and you feel more comfortable with them.

Using the book

You could probably work through the whole book in a single day, but there is a good deal in it so it is better to take one chapter, or even part of a chapter, at a time, giving yourself a chance to reflect on that before moving on. Working out and following up the implications of possible solutions to problems may of course take a lot longer, and involve discussions with students and colleagues. Evaluating the effects of those changes will take longer still, but it is important to try to do this and gather some evidence about the effectiveness of the various approaches and techniques you employ.

The three chapters correspond to three increasingly broad levels of analysis: the teaching session, the course or programme, and the institution. Most people will need to work through them in that order, although if your main concern is with the design and organization of courses or modules you can begin with Chapter 2, and if you are primarily a manager of teaching you can go straight to Chapter 3. However the book is designed from the ground up, as it were, so it is useful to read through all the chapters even if you do not respond to them. Likewise, even if your responsibilities are limited to classroom teaching, it may be useful for you to understand some of the issues involved in course planning, provision and management. Teaching does not take place in a vacuum, and what happens in the classroom, laboratory or lecture hall is shaped in both obvious and subtle ways by the context in which it takes place.

If you teach on a variety of courses or programmes you will need to choose *one* on which to base your analysis, and within that to focus on certain sessions or classes. It is important to respond in terms of concrete experiences and actual examples. These will probably throw up broader, general questions about your work, but if you think your teaching situation is radically different in other classes or courses, you can work through the chapters a second time with a different example in mind. Often the difference between two situations can be illuminating in itself, not least in how we respond to them.

Read the introduction to each chapter. This is quite short but explains the basis for the questions in that chapter. It is important not simply to respond to questions but to understand why they are being asked, and also in what ways they may be related to one another. Although the book is organized in terms of 35 discrete sections, in reality these will often interact with and impact on one another. In order to trouble-shoot we need to break teaching down into these distinct aspects, but finding effective solutions will often involve not one but several of them. Indeed the solution to one problem may give rise to another, so sometimes we have to look for the best compromise or trade-off that we can find.

Each chapter consists of a number of short sections, which you should work through as follows:

Step One

Respond to the initial key question by ticking NO, the question mark (?) or YES. If you are not sure what the question means or how to respond, read the short paragraph and trigger questions that follow and then respond to it. Ring NO if your response is mainly or completely negative. Ring the question mark if you are undecided or your response is mixed, for example: 'partly', 'some of the time', 'in some cases', or 'up to a point'. Ring YES if your response is mainly or wholly positive. If your response is YES, you can go straight on to the next section, although you will still probably find something of interest or use in the current one. If your response is a query or negative, work through the other steps as follows.

Step Two

If you haven't done so already, read the introductory paragraph and then think about the list of trigger questions that follows. Highlight or underline the ones that seem particularly relevant. You may think of others to add. Then read the rest of the text below, which sets out the main ideas related to that topic.

Step Three

Identify the problem or problems in the response box below. Try to pinpoint the reasons, and any related problems or issues. Do this in brief, note form but in enough detail to be comprehensible to others or yourself if you return to it sometime later. Use your own notepad if you want to go into more detail, in this or other boxes, which vary in length because of pagination.

Step Four

Read down the list of possible solutions. These may not solve the problem entirely and may simply represent a way of coping with it or preventing it from getting worse, but they do form a range of actions that you can consider. They tend to be typical, general solutions and if you can think up others that fit your own particular situation better, do not hesitate to add them. Use your common sense and professional judgement in evaluating your options.

Step Five

Note down your proposed solution or solutions in the box provided. There may be one main action you plan to take, or a cluster of related measures. Sometimes the solution will involve a general strategy or shift of approach that then has to be implemented in various ways. Sometimes there will be nothing you can do. We are not in complete control of our teaching. To begin with, it is a consenting activity that depends on the cooperation of students; no one can force people to learn. We operate within a system that limits us in terms of regulations and resources. We are part of a society that has certain norms and expectations. So trouble-shooting may throw up dilemmas as well as solutions. That is not a comforting thought, but at least this kind of analysis will help you to see what your position really is. In other cases, you may identify an obvious solution but be constrained by lack of time or money, or you may decide that it will not work with your particular students or colleagues. Your proposed solutions will form the basis of your action plan at the end of each chapter, and you will need to refer back to them when you get there.

When you have completed all these steps, go on to the next section. As you respond to each initial question, ask yourself: how do I know? What evidence do I have for my response? The final question in each chapter is: anything else? This allows you to add any problems that have not been analysed adequately in the previous sections and that may stem from the particular circumstances of your own work. A book such as this cannot hope to cover all eventualities and you should not hesitate to include issues that seem important to you or your colleagues.

At the end of each chapter you will find a profile of responses that you can fill in, this time using a seven-point scale. You will need to check back on each section as you do so, and this will allow you to re-evaluate your initial response in the light of both the analysis and the subsequent sections. The results will create a useful profile of that aspect of your work – session, course, management – that you can reflect on and compare with those of your colleagues. On the following page there is a form for you to summarize the main actions arising out of your analysis that you can use as an agenda for discussion or as a 'contract' with yourself.

Bear in mind some general points when you devise your action plan. First, some problems may be temporary or short term. For example, there can be teething troubles at the beginning of a course that sort themselves out over time. In other cases, the problem may relate to a particular group of students and not others. New administrative arrangements can take time to bed down. Be wary of over-reacting to immediate problems, and perhaps seek the advice of older or more experienced staff who have been through this kind of thing before.

Second, most solutions will involve other people. There are some changes we can make within the confines of our own class that do not affect other staff, though they will affect the students, and may depend on their expectations, abilities and attitudes. However, teaching is in the main a collaborative activity, so it is essential that you bear your colleagues, including ancillary or support staff, in mind.

Third, remember to consider carefully the legal and ethical aspects of any changes you propose. Teaching typically involves an imbalance of power between teacher and student, not simply in the teaching–learning process but in the assessment of it, and is carried out (rightly) within a legal and regulatory framework designed primarily to protect the learner. It also involves ethical concepts and standards associated with the very idea of education. We must avoid infringing the first or undermining the second.

Your own role

Teaching is not just what goes on in the classroom: it is everything we do to facilitate student learning. Therefore the initial analysis of the classroom session in Chapter 1 broadens out in Chapter 2 to cover the design, organization and assessment of the course as a whole, and the management of all this in Chapter 3.

The way you respond to each chapter will depend on the kind of institution you teach in, and your own role within it. It may be useful therefore right at the start to analyse your situation in terms of the type of institution you work in and the degree of control you have over your teaching. Educational institutions range from the hierarchical to the collegial. The first are vertical organizations, with many of the features of the stereotypical bureaucracy: well-defined levels, clearly demarcated roles, specified channels of communication and a top-down chain of command. These levels correspond broadly to the three levels of analysis in the book: teachers teach, course leaders lead courses, and managers manage. By contrast, collegial organizations are complaratively flat and often less structured; informal networks, relationships and channels may be relatively more important. Most decisions are taken by individuals or groups of colleagues, often in committees or assemblies (such as a university senate), and there are overlapping and sometimes blurred roles; the same person may teach, lead courses and manage.

Most educational institutions comprise a mixture of the hierarchical and collegial, but the balance varies not only from one sector to another, but between and even within institutions. Thus while further education colleges tend to be relatively hierarchical, and universities relatively collegial, there are considerable differences between one institution (or department) and the next. Where would you place your institution on this dimension?

The second dimension is the degree of control you have over your own teaching. Do you design your courses or follow a laid-down curriculum? Do you create your own materials or use prescribed textbooks? Do you have a say in who comes on your course? Are you free to teach as you want? Who sets and marks assignments or exams? Who inspects or evaluates? How far are any of the above under your control, or subject to external – perhaps even national – regulation? Does the answer vary in terms of curriculum, materials, methods or assessment? While teachers in schools and colleges are generally reckoned to be less autonomous than their counterparts in higher or adult education, recent changes in the latter sectors have led to an increase in external regulation in the name of accountability, consistency and the maintenance of standards.

Try placing yourself (with an X) somewhere in Figure 0.1. This should help you to respond to the questions in each chapter, and to reflect on your own role in the institution. You may, however, need to return to this diagram several times as you progress through the book. You may find that you have more or less control than you thought, or that the locus of control has shifted, or that changes in the organizational structure or culture – in terms of the hierarchical/collegial balance – have affected your role and the way you do your job.

There are four appendices at the end of the book. The first two (*What's going on?* and *Whose job is it anyway?*) suggest practical activities for exploring the process of classroom teaching and learning, and the relative responsibilities of teacher and student in it. The third appendix has some brief *Guidelines for workshop leaders* who want to use this book, or parts of it, in organized staff development events. The final appendix is *A note for foreign readers*.

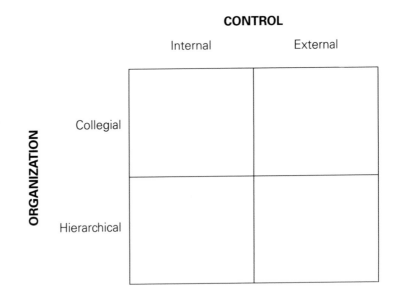

CONTROL

Internal   External

Collegial

ORGANIZATION

Hierarchical

Figure 0.1 *Your teaching environment*

Following the appendices you will find *Further reading* and *Notes*, which set out briefly the theoretical basis of this approach and provide some additional references. While you can use the book without reading these sections, it is important to understand the thinking behind this analysis, if only so that you can identify and perhaps question the assumptions involved. Each of the chapters is based on an underlying model of teaching or management, which in turn stems from a general theory of professional activity. This has been set out in detail in a series of publications that are listed in this section. Suggestions for further reading on some other topics (indicated by 'see Notes' in the text) are also given.

It should have become clear by now that this is a book not simply to read but to work through and with. The book itself depends on a partnership between author and reader. It relies heavily on your reflections and responses. It does not offer prescribed solutions, because it is impossible to do so in blanket, general terms. It does however provide a framework that will help you identify and then address any problems you may be having. And it should be of interest even if you are not having any.

Such a framework takes us back to the whole idea of trouble-shooting. It was pointed out at the beginning that trouble-shooting in teaching is by no means as neat or well-defined a process as it can be in a technical field, and some people may think it too mechanistic or impersonal a term to use about a human activity such as teaching. The opposite problem however is that some teachers see their work entirely in personal terms – as an extension of themselves – and attribute everything that happens to their own behaviour. One of the challenges of teaching is that we have to be involved in it to do it well and yet detached from it to see what we are doing. Not everything that goes wrong is our fault, and not everything that goes well is down to us either. If the framework set out here helps you to strike some balance between involvement in and detachment from your work, then it will have fulfilled its emotional, as well as cognitive, purpose.

At first sight, a title such as *Trouble-shooting your Teaching* may seem a bit negative. However, if anything, it is the opposite. You will probably find that many of the aspects of your teaching that are explored in this book work reasonably well, and some very well. By isolating and identifying those that do not, we can turn an already satisfactory activity into a really good and satisfying one. This book will help you to focus your attention and concentrate your energies on those areas where they are most needed, and where they are most likely to bring improvements for both you and your students.

Trouble-shooting the session

Introduction

This first chapter focuses on the analysis of the teaching session. This covers not only the typical school class or lesson, but any form of organized teaching event such as a workshop, seminar, lecture, laboratory period, practical class or field trip. It also covers individual or small group tutoring, supervision or coaching.

One teaching session can differ a good deal from another. For your analysis, choose one or more sessions that you think are fairly typical or represent-ative of your work. The aim of this chapter is to engage in a concrete, 'grounded' analysis of some actual teaching, rather than try to generalize about your experience, so if some of your teaching sessions are very different it is best to go through the chapter a second or third time, using other examples. The contrasts between the various situations should in themselves throw up interesting questions.

In one way, the session is the obvious place to start. It is the crucible of teaching, where it happens. At the same time, any analysis of a class or session will quickly show that we cannot treat it in isolation, not just from other classes but from other elements of teaching and learning. Students may need to prepare for the session and there will often be follow-up work as well. One session may relate to or lead on to another. The work that is done in them all will be assessed. Teaching comes as a package; it is not just a single event, but a combination of different kinds of activities that together comprise the environment for learning. In responding to the questions that follow, therefore, you should bear in mind not simply what happens (or does not happen) during the actual event but what precedes, surrounds and follows it. Indeed the problem trail may lead you away from the session itself towards these related or contextual issues.

Teaching functions

The first six questions deal with six mainly cognitive functions of teaching (see Notes). Each of these is explored in detail in the sections that follow but in simple terms they are:

- *Audit:* finding out and building on what the learners already know or can do.
- *Orientation:* establishing a sense of direction or agenda for learning.
- *Input:* providing or eliciting the content or subject matter.
- *Explanation:* ensuring that the learners understand what they are learning.
- *Setting tasks:* creating activities for learners to apply or try out their learning.
- *Giving feedback:* reporting back to the learners on their performance.

If you sit in on a class you can often observe these six functions occurring in this order (both 'task' and 'feedback' are being used as verbs here):

Audit → Orient → Input → Explain → Task → Feedback

This forms a quite common, logical sequence of teaching: first look back at what the students have done before, then look forward to what they should do, then provide the necessary inputs, and so on. However, this is by no means a universal pattern. For example, you may (rightly or wrongly) assume that there is no need to *audit* the students' prior learning because you know what they did previously (are you sure?). You might deliberately avoid *orienting* them because you want them to explore or discover the possibilities for themselves. Problem-based learning tends to begin with the *task*, on the grounds that this provides a concrete, motivating point of departure, and uses that to draw in the previous functions. *Explanation* may come not only before the task but after in the form of explanatory *feedback*. The order and relationship of these six functions differs from one situation to another; it all depends on what you are teaching, to whom, where and of course why.

Teaching and learning are not however purely cognitive enterprises. They do not happen unless people want to do them, and keep doing them. So the next three sections deal with three *affective* or emotional functions:

- *Motivation:* creating the will to embark on and sustain learning.
- *Belief:* developing the conviction that one can learn.
- *Reward:* providing or realizing the benefits of learning.

Whereas one can often pin down a cognitive function in the class at the moment it is happening (eg, now the teacher is *orienting* the group/giving *feedback* to that particular student), the affective functions are more subtle and diffuse. We can sometimes watch a teacher trying to enthuse a class about a new topic, and we can hear him or her praising a group or trying to bolster the confidence of an individual. However, the affective or emotional side of teaching is more often a matter of atmosphere or tone, something we pick up from teachers' and students' behaviour, the ethos of the class, the general 'vibes'. Often, we can only really get at it by talking to students on an individual basis to find out what interests them or whether they think they can actually cope with the course. The elusiveness of affect (emotions, feelings, attitudes, self-image) should not however deter us from exploring this side of teaching and learning, since it drives the whole activity. Without a measure of motivation, self-belief and reward, little learning will take place.

People often refer to 'learning' as if it was a self-evident concept, as if we all knew what it was. However, the last two functions address precisely this point. They are:

- *Exploration:* probing the scope or nature of what one is learning.
- *Reflection:* thinking about one's own learning process.

Many classes and indeed courses downplay or even disregard these two remaining functions, perhaps because they seem too abstract, intangible or 'airy-fairy'. Such teaching is concerned simply to get on with the job, without ever considering the nature of that job or what getting on with it means. But learning is not a simple or self-evident idea; it has to be interpreted by those involved, and there are many different ways of doing this (see Notes). The way teachers and learners view learning affects how they go about it, indeed what they think it is; for example, where one student will construe learning as memorizing, another will see it in terms of understanding or applying; where one will adopt a passive approach, another may be much more proactive. The way a student views learning defines what it means to be a student; and that can sometimes be the root of the problem. So although the nine cognitive and affective functions cover most aspects of teaching and learning, we need to add another level of thinking about those functions: meta-cognition and meta-affect. In simple terms, these involve some degree of awareness about one's own knowing and feeling, and this consciousness will affect one's approach to learning and the strategies one employs. While these general issues may not always surface in a particular class or session, it is important to consider them in the light of the longer-term development of the student.

The teaching–learning triangle

The three kinds of function – cognitive, affective and meta-cognitive/affective – are related. The cognitive functions may have an affective tinge, the affective functions will have some cognitive content, and the meta-level functions relate back to the other two. It is useful therefore to see all three in terms of the triangle in Figure 1.1. At any given time, you may be more concerned with one point of the triangle than the others, but it is important to bear in mind the overall picture. Different classes tend to throw up different problems and you will probably need to explore most of the eleven functions at one time or another in your work. And we should not let the more immediate cognitive and affective problems, which tend to preoccupy our attention, marginalize the longer-term, 'meta' ones: after all, education is a lifelong business and we all have a responsibility for the development of the learner over time.

By working through the various questions in Chapter 1 you will be able to trouble-shoot your teaching at the level of the class or session and diagnose any problems that you are having. However, you may have a vague sense that something is wrong or not quite right, but be unable to put your finger on it, even after such an analysis. Or you may simply want to get a broad feel for the nature and dynamics of your sessions. There are two appendices at the end of the book that will help you to do this. The first (Appendix 1) explains how to observe and analyse a session in terms of not just functions but variables and methods as well, using a three-dimensional framework. This will give you a detailed picture of 'what's going on' in your class. It is best done with a colleague (each of you observes the other) and involves some close observation and subsequent discussion, but it will give you a general view of your teaching that may help place any specific problems in perspective. Appendix 2 (*Whose job is it anyway?*) provides a tool for analysing the relative responsibilities of teacher and student for

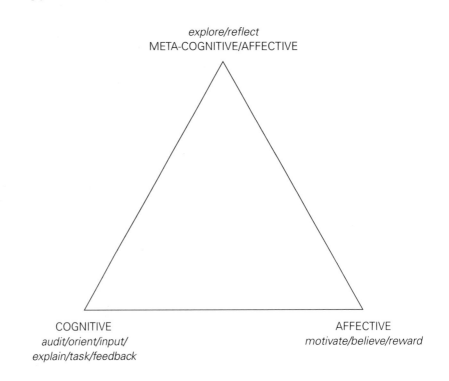

explore/reflect
META-COGNITIVE/AFFECTIVE

COGNITIVE
audit/orient/input/
explain/task/feedback

AFFECTIVE
motivate/believe/reward

Figure 1.1   *The teaching–learning triangle*

the functions set out in this chapter. It can be used with your colleagues or students as a means of exploring people's interpretations of their roles and the extent to which these expectations coincide.

Please turn now to Section 1, and begin your analysis. If necessary, refer back to pages 4–5 for instructions on the steps to follow in each section.

1 DOES YOUR TEACHING BUILD ON THE STUDENTS' PREVIOUS LEARNING?

NO ☐   ? ☐   YES ☐

Both at the level of the course and the class, teaching needs to take account of what the students have done before, so this first question is about the relationship between your teaching and what the students bring to the sessions by way of existing knowledge, skills and attitudes. In some cases, they may be embarking on a quite new subject or topic that seems to involve little or no prior knowledge, though even then the slate is not quite clean: there may well be related skills or ideas that affect their learning. At the other extreme, prior knowledge, skills or experience may actually block or interfere with their new learning, and have to be 'unlearned' before they can progress. Whatever the situation, you will need to consider where they are coming from.

- Do you know what your students have done before?
- Is your teaching meant to build on what they covered in previous sessions?
- Are your sessions meant to dovetail with other ones?
- Are you sometimes surprised at the type or level of questions students ask?
- Have they got a solid foundation for what they are doing now?
- Are there any obvious gaps in their existing knowledge or skills?
- How homogeneous is the group in terms of prior learning or experience?
- Are there any signs of previous learning impeding new learning?

One way of thinking about this is in terms of *baselines*. Where do I start from? What can I assume about the students? That in turn depends on where your teaching fits into the wider picture. It may be part of a planned sequence of development in which A leads to B, which then leads on to C; if so continuity is essential. On the other hand it may have only a loose or indirect relationship with what has gone before.

The degree of continuity will also differ from subject to subject. Some subjects such as mathematics, computing, languages and the natural sciences are generally regarded as linear; others, such as history, literature or art, may form a looser network of related topics or themes. What is your subject like?

You might expect the problems of foundations or continuity to be greatest where courses are stand-alone. This would be true of many training situations where a programme or workshop brings together participants whom the trainer has never set eyes on before. However, even in the more consecutive education system, where there is meant to be progression from one year or level to the next, we can get problems because we assume that something has been covered whereas in fact it has not, or the students have not really grasped it. (And most teachers have to plan their courses before they actually meet the students.) The growth of modular systems also means that you may have students who have done a variety of previous courses.

Baseline problems can also arise for more practical reasons. Some students may have missed previous sessions. If you are taking over a class from another teacher you might find it difficult to know exactly what the class has done. If the class does not meet frequently you may need to remind the students (and yourself) what was covered last time in order to cue them in again and provide continuity. Pressure of time and a lot to get through may mean that you do not establish the learners' baselines as carefully as you should.

The problem of prior learning inhibiting new ways of understanding is most common on post-experience courses where people bring a stock of well-established habits, skills or attitudes to the situation. This is most obvious in the area of skills; for example, it can be very difficult to change the way you drive or play golf after a long time. More generally, students may bring with them a whole array of ideas and values that are bound up with their own sense of identity. And we all have implicit theories about the world – what causes X, the reasons for Y – that may conflict with the formal theories we are taught.

One final point. We have been talking as if prior learning was typically a problem. However, it can also provide a positive agenda for new learning, if you want to start with the students' experience and use this as the point of departure for planning your class. In that case, you will need to have a number of potential 'scripts' in mind that you can use and develop as the need arises. For this reason, student-centred teaching can require more, not less, preparation than a pre-planned didactic approach.

Note down the main problem or problems you face in the box below.

WHAT'S THE PROBLEM?

Here are some things you can try, depending on the situation:

- Set a diagnostic test at the beginning of the class to find out what the level of knowledge or skills really is. It is generally easier to do this in more precise subjects such as languages, mathematics or computing, or with practical or performance skills. However, you may be able to devise simple tests in other subjects that will give you some feel for what the students know. Or you can set a short, early assignment that does not count towards final assessment.
- Give the students a simple checklist or questionnaire to find out what they know/have done already. This will allow you to establish not only the general baseline but individual exceptions to it.
- Begin the class with a general discussion about the topic and ask specific questions that will help you assess the level of prior knowledge (Have you come across. . .? Did you cover. . .?). However, be careful not to take this entirely at face value since students may not want to show their ignorance (or knowledge) in front of a new group.
- You can start any session with a brief review of the last one and invite any remaining questions about it (is everyone happy about. . .?), but that can cut into the amount of time you have to cover what you intended and you will need to judge how long to

spend going over the ground again. On the other hand, there is no point going on if students really do not understand the previous step or stage.

- If you have a class of mature, adult students, ask them about their relevant experience. Not only will this give you a feel for where they are, it will indicate that you value what they bring to the situation and allow you to draw on it if the opportunity arises.
- Log any persistent problems that seem to stem from a lack of prior learning, and see if you can trace them back to source, for example in a previous class or year. You may need to talk to colleagues about this.
- If the problems affect individual students, try to find time to talk to them one to one, perhaps after the class. If there are useful back-up or remedial materials, provide them or advise students where to find them.
- If the problem concerns a number of students, try to organize some extra, catch-up sessions for them, if time and money allow. Remember (and remind them) that it is not their fault that they missed out.
- If there is a wider mismatch between your teaching and the prior learning of the group, you will need to look at the whole selection or admission process. This is an issue that goes well beyond your own class and will involve colleagues and course managers. (See Section 12.)
- A quite different problem arises when some students have covered the ground already and do not want to go over it again. Try to find alternative work or activities for them to get on with individually while you deal with the main group.
- Where students have in fact learned much of what you are teaching through prior study or experience, it may be worth setting up a system for accrediting prior learning (APL) if one does not already exist. However, be warned that this is a time-consuming and quite complex, though educative, process for both staff and students, and not all students will be able to cope with it.
- If possible, get more background information on your new students from records and files or those who have taught them before. But be careful that this does not lead you to prejudge their potential; teachers' expectations can influence students' performance and turn into a self-fulfilling prophecy (the 'Pygmalion effect'; see Notes).

● Last but not least, you may need to review your own teaching plans for the class. Be prepared to invest/waste some time early on establishing the right baseline; it will pay off later.

Note down any potential solutions in the box below.

SOLUTIONS

Decide which course of action is likely to be most effective and most practicable, and highlight or underline it so that you can refer to it easily again when you look back over the chapter. Please turn now to Section 2.

2 DO THE STUDENTS KNOW WHERE THEY ARE GOING?

NO ☐   **?** ☐   **YES** ☐

Learning involves not only understanding where one is coming from but where one is going. On the whole, students learn better if they have some sense of direction. This allows them to concentrate their attention and focus their efforts on what they should know or be able to do by the end of the learning event. For this reason, teachers and trainers are usually advised to identify the objectives or intended learning outcomes of their sessions and share these with the students at the beginning. Such object-ives also allow students to break down large learning tasks into more manageable and less daunting stages. In general terms, we can say that the teacher needs to orient his or her students, both at the level of the course and the class, although that advice has to be qualified in various ways that will be spelled out below. However, orientation remains a good, general principle that you need to have equally good reasons for ignoring.

- Do your students show any signs of feeling disoriented?
- Do you get frequent questions about what they are meant to do or how they are meant to go about it?
- Is it appropriate to specify objectives for each session or merely to have general aims for the course as a whole?
- Should the aims and objectives be prescribed or negotiated?
- Is your subject well defined or open ended?
- Do you prefer to teach in a planned or spontaneous way?
- Do your teaching objectives tally with the assessment criteria? (See Section 23.)

Learning does not have to be goal-directed. When people learn inform-ally, under their own control, they may not identify any aims or goals at all but proceed incrementally or opportunistically; one thing leads to another and the solution to one problem becomes the point of departure for the next (see Notes). Learning can be evolutionary, and this is important within formal settings too if we are trying to encourage curiosity or enquiry. Outcomes may focus students' attention, but they can also inhibit learning around the topic, something implicit in the idea of 'reading for a degree' and central to the ethos of liberal adult education. A less structured agenda also allows the teacher to take up useful points as they occur, to exploit interesting tangents and generally to ride on the momentum of discussion. It gives students a sense that they can shape the direction of their learning, and perhaps helps them to identify with it and 'own' it more strongly. Teachers can do too much as well as too little for students. Indeed, thinking through the purpose of one's own learning is an integral part of some higher levels of learning.

Having said this, students on the majority of courses and in the majority of classes benefit from some sense of orientation, some structure or map that allows them to see where they are and where they should be going. That need varies from student to student, subject to subject and setting to setting. It may even vary at different stages of a course; for example, you may find that the initial need for structure and security gradually gives way to a more confident, free-ranging approach.

The need for clear, precise objectives is probably greatest in skill-based subjects where it is important to specify exactly what students should be able to do, for example in terms of job competences or safe practice. However, even in more general subjects, you should not assume that all students will know what is expected; that kind of tacit knowledge often depends on social and educational background, and in any case some students are better at picking up cues than others. You will probably also find that some students seem to need more structure or freedom than others, and you have to judge just much how is optimum in each case: too much structure can encourage a dependence on you or the materials, which may in turn inhibit students' capacity to develop their potential and think for themselves.

Although it is not always easy to specify outcomes for knowledge/under-standing and skills, particularly at the higher levels, there exist taxonomies for doing this that can act as a template (see Notes). But do some of your aims and objectives concern *attitudes* and *values*? For example, do you want to encourage critical thinking, individual responsibility or creativity, or the capacity to work in a team? Is your teaching concerned with changing the students' view of themselves, their roles or the organization or society they work and live in? To what extent are such aims implicit or explicit, part of the 'hidden curriculum' (see Notes) or the subject of explicit discussion?

Recently, a great deal of emphasis in post-compulsory education has been placed on what are variously called core, key, generic or transferable skills (see Notes). These may relate to concrete competences such as communication, numeracy and computer literacy, but they may also embrace wider notions such as initiative, team working, time management, problem solving and creativity. There are several questions to consider. First, are these really skills in the usual sense of the word, or do they involve cognition and attitudes as well? Second, are you sure that they are actually transferable from one context to another? Third, are they appropriate aims for your teaching? And if so, should you teach them in stand-alone courses or try to embed them in other subject matter?

Finally, it is important to remember that orientation may be general or specific. The first assumes that students can translate broad aims or goals into more concrete or intermediate targets for themselves; historically, most courses operated on this basis and there was little or no attempt to spell out precise objectives. The second assumes that students can see the common principles or general aims in a long and perhaps fragmented list of specific objectives. Which is your approach? And how do you know that it works?

Note down any problems that concern you.

WHAT'S THE PROBLEM?

Here are some possible solutions to problems of orientation:

- Discuss the overall course plan with the group. Try to find out if they are experiencing too much or too little orientation.
- If the latter, write specific objectives or intended learning outcomes for each session and set them out on an acetate or on paper at the beginning. Refer back to the course handbook if they are listed there.
- For these objectives to be really precise, they should specify (i) what the student should be able to do, (ii) to what level or standard and (iii) in what conditions (time, access to materials, environment).
- Incorporate objectives or outcomes into handouts so that the students know what the material is for.
- Organize the class into small groups and ask them to identify the aims of the course or objectives of the class (What do you think we should cover?). Then relate these to the formal aims.
- If the students feel the course is too rigid, explore ways you can free it up, perhaps by trying to cover less or varying the amount of time you allocate to each topic. This may in turn have implications for assessment.
- Continually relate what you are covering in the class to assignments or assessment, so that the students can see the connection. However, you may not want to tie in everything you do to assessment, since this can over-focus or narrow the students' approach.
- If particular students seem to be disoriented, try to spend some time with them individually, explaining the structure and direction of the course.
- Talk to colleagues to see if they are having similar problems. It may be that the programme as a whole is ill defined or poorly structured, in which case you will need to act together to remedy the situation.
- If it seems appropriate, recap at the end of each session. Summarize or synthesize what you covered and give some pointers to the next session, as 'advance organizers' (see Notes).
- Review where you have got to and where you are going about half way through the course. Re-orient the students at each major new stage.

List any practical solutions in the box below.

SOLUTIONS

Having worked through this section, you might want to check your initial response again to see if you still hold to it. Then move on to Section 3.

3 ARE THE STUDENTS GETTING THE INPUTS THEY NEED?

NO ☐   ? ☐   YES ☐

Learning is learning about something. It has to have some substance, some content. Another way of putting this is to say that it involves the processing of information, so long as we use 'information' to cover anything that one might learn or learn about: concepts, values, skills, approaches, strategies, as well as facts or data. Such inputs may come directly from the teacher, through presentation and demonstration, or indirectly through materials such as books, videos, handouts and software. It may come from structured experiences such as practical experiments, workshops and performances, field trips or placements. And we should not forget that it may also come from the students, as they make their own experience available to themselves and others as material for their learning (see Appendix 2). The question is: are there sufficient inputs, from all these different sources, for the students to work on?

- Is the content of your own presentations/demonstrations OK?
- Is the delivery of your own presentations/demonstrations OK?
- Are you satisfied with the quality of the learning resources and materials?
- Are there any problems of access to such resources?
- What about the quality of the other learning inputs or experiences?
- Is enough use made of the students' own potential contributions?
- Have the students the skills they need to make use of all these inputs?
- Do they actually make use of them?

Traditional definitions of teaching usually include some reference to 'imparting knowledge'. Words like *impart* and *input* imply a rather one-way 'transmission' theory of teaching (clean slates, blank sheets, empty vessels and the like), which, as many of the other sections in this book will make clear, is inadequate and potentially misleading. However, they do point to the need for some kind of stimulus for learning, whether that comes from external sources or from the learners themselves. Such inputs or stimuli are then mentally processed in various ways and lead to 'outputs' or responses in the form of what the students say, write or do. This model of teaching and learning is open to the objection that students' cognitive frameworks filter or pre-select the very stimuli they perceive, so the idea of input is itself problematic. But the model remains useful in focusing our attention on what is presented or made available to the students in the first place (see Notes).

Input problems subdivide into those of content and delivery. The teaching should be comprehensive and cover everything that is necessary. All the topics should receive adequate treatment. It should also be (as appropriate) accurate, informed, up to date, unbiased and relevant. Those qualities tend to apply to organized bodies of knowledge. However, even where the teaching draws mainly on the students' own experience or thinking, there should be enough 'material' there for them to work on. Input problems tend to arise when the content is unbalanced or incomplete, when teachers do not know their stuff, when the materials are patchy, when the equipment is out of date, or when the range of resources is limited. They typically result in students feeling that the course is a bit superficial or thin, somehow lacking in substance, or that it does not really do justice to the subject.

Even if the substance is there, it needs the teacher to put it across or draw it out. This requires skills of presentation, demonstration and questioning. Likewise, even if the content of the materials is adequate, they need to be designed, written and presented in such a way that students can use them effectively. This is not to say that they should be easy or 'dumbed down', but simply that the presentation (or lack of it) does not get in the way. Audio-visual materials and computer software in particular need to be designed to be user-friendly, otherwise the problems of accessing them divert the students' attention away from their content.

However, even if both content and delivery are OK, problems can arise if the students do not have the skills or the motivation to use them. The best presentation is wasted if the students are not listening. The best written materials are useless if the students do not read them. Strictly speaking, this is not a problem of input but it appears as such in terms of lack of detail or depth in seminars and discussions or lack of substance in essays and reports. Where the 'content' of the teaching derives from the students' own experience and know-how this is less likely to be a problem, but they still have to be ready to make it available to themselves and others through reflection and analysis.

Finally, cultural variables may affect this aspect of teaching. In some cultures and systems, teachers are imbued with great authority precisely because they dispense knowledge in the form of input, and much less value is placed on the students' contribution; indeed, there may be considerable resistance to the idea of group discussion and peer-learning precisely because the students are 'merely' students: after all, they are there to learn. In other cultures, by contrast, the student is looked upon as a valuable source of ideas and experience and seen as a genuine partner in the process. Are you aware of such cultural differences in the groups you teach? And what is your view? In what ways has it been shaped by your own previous experience as a student? And how far do your colleagues share it?

Note down these or any other problems related to input that concern you.

WHAT'S THE PROBLEM?

Here are some things you might try:

- Check the design of each session to see that it is neither light-weight nor overloaded. Both of these can cause input problems, the first because it is incomplete, the second because it tends to lead to 'surface' learning (ie, memorization and regurgitation) rather than 'deep' learning (real understanding). See also Section 4 for more on this.
- Courses often grow incrementally without our noticing as we add more and more interesting or desirable things to them without taking anything out. (Professional bodies are also sometimes guilty of this.) Divide your course into *must teach/should teach/could teach* and redesign it accordingly. That should take off some of the pressure to get through things in the class.
- Check what you cover in class against the pattern of assessment. Does it map properly onto the latter in terms of both scope and level? (See also Sections 23 and 24).
- Discuss with the group what they know about the topic already and see how best you can incorporate that as input.
- If students find some texts particularly difficult, try giving them an initial briefing before they tackle them.
- Check your learning materials and if necessary revise them; they may have a limited shelf life. This is a routine, ongoing process that needs to be done regularly.
- You may need to update yourself by going on courses/workshops, talking to colleagues or doing some reading.
- If there are major gaps in materials, try to locate new ones. If you cannot, or they do not exist, create some for your own use. You may be able to tap into some development funds to do this.
- Ask a colleague to sit in on your class and focus on your present-ations/demonstrations. Are they clear? Audible? Well structured? Well paced? Interesting?
- Find out which parts of the course the students 'got most from': presentations, materials, practical sessions, private study, and so on. Explore the reasons why.
- Check that the students have the skills they need to make use of the various inputs. If not, spend some time in the class going over these or organize special workshops (see also Section 17).
- Try to explore general attitudes to input, knowledge, expertise and authority with the group. These are big issues, so it is probably best

not to tackle them head on, but to open them up spontaneously as the occasion arises. (See also Sections 10 and 11.)

Note down any likely answers to input problems.

SOLUTIONS

This section and the next are closely linked and need to be taken together.

4 DO THE STUDENTS UNDERSTAND WHAT THEY ARE LEARNING?

NO ☐   **?** ☐   **YES** ☐

The fact that the words 'learn' and 'understand' are sometimes treated as interchangeable indicates just how central the latter is to teaching. True, there is an element of rote learning of facts, words, names or formulae in most fields, and skill learning consists in the building up and mastery of techniques and routines. It may also be difficult to articulate just what kind of learning is going on in some of the creative or performing arts, which seem to involve more tacit forms of knowledge. But most subjects and topics require the learners to follow, grasp or make sense of content in a way that then allows them to work with, re-construct or apply it in some fashion. And this understanding enables them to internalize it, to make it their own, to embed it in their cognitive worlds. Interaction is the key to this process.

- Do students in the class frequently say 'I don't follow that' or 'Could you go over that again?' or something similar?
- Do you get the feeling (perhaps from their silence or faces) that they haven't got the hang of it?
- Do they ask questions or give responses that imply that they have got the wrong end of the stick?
- When you set problems or exercises are they simply beyond some students?
- Does students' written work tend to describe or reproduce what you have said rather than use or apply it in some way?
- Do they see exams primarily as a test of memory? Does their approach to learning change as they get nearer the exams?
- How important is 'understanding' as an aim in your teaching? How important is it to the students? Do your expectations coincide?

Not all forms of learning are the same. Indeed, learning is best seen as an 'umbrella concept' that can cover anything from absorbing a fresh piece of information or acquiring a new skill, through grasping patterns and relationships or developing new concepts or strategies, to changing the whole way we see ourselves, others and the world. The relative emphasis on each of these different kinds of learning will depend on the sort of course you teach. The first thing therefore is to decide what kind of learning you want to promote, and the second is to ensure that all the elements of your teaching – content, methods, materials, style and above all assessment – are consistent with one another in promoting that learning.

That said, the idea of understanding has often been seen as the defining aspect of education, and although in the past it was less important in the narrower forms of training, it has now become critical there as well. While if we learn merely how to perform certain techniques or procedures, without understanding them, we will be lost if something goes wrong or we have to transfer them to a different context or problem. Understanding thus underpins adaptability in the world of work as elsewhere.

The extent to which students understand what they are learning is therefore usually a central measure of the success of teaching, with the corollary that one of the key functions of teachers is to 'explain things' and help students when they 'get stuck'. Explaining is not just a one-way process, and when someone says 'I explained the stock market crash to the class this morning' the response should be: '*How do you know?*' Explaining involves relating the cognitive world of the subject (or teacher) to that of the learner and checking that this has actually been accomplished. Much of the time we may rely on students figuring things out for themselves but even the best students sometimes run into a problem that needs unblocking.

One problem is that teachers sometimes simply present a topic (see the previous section on Input) and then move straight on to a task without pausing to make sure that the students have really understood it. This sometimes reflects pressure of time and the need to cover a lot of ground; large classes also make checking understanding difficult. And when a student does ask a question, one has to balance the desire to respond with the need to keep the group's attention and momentum. A different and more serious problem is that students may view learning as mainly a matter of memorizing and reproducing what they have been taught rather than making sense of it for themselves: 'surface learning' rather than 'deep learning' (see Notes). This may reflect their own preferred or habitual approach but it may also be the result of the messages they pick up from the teaching environment. Do the lecturers or teachers project such an attitude? Does the curriculum require it? Do the materials exemplify it?

Does the assessment reinforce it? Students can take their cue from all these aspects of teaching, especially the last, which for them is the 'bottom line'.

Note down the key problems below.

WHAT'S THE PROBLEM?

Here are some solutions to consider:

- Focus on the way you ask and answer questions. In particular, note what you do when students say that they do not understand or follow something. Break it down into smaller steps or stages? Look for an example, parallel or analogy? Translate it into language they will understand? Encourage the student to articulate the nature of the problem? Ask another student to explain it? If necessary, get a colleague to sit in and listen to how you do all this.

- Build questions into handouts. These will encourage students to engage with the material actively rather than just absorbing it passively.
- Begin a session with a few key questions. Then use the rest of the time to answer or explore them. Return to them at the end.
- Look carefully at the kinds of comments you make on written work. Do they really help the student to understand? Or are they just token ticks, underlinings or question marks? The way you comment on work affects the student's approach to learning.
- Find simpler or more basic texts that weaker students can use as a backup to the standard ones in areas of difficulty.
- If your timetable allows, set aside some individual tutorial sessions to help students who seem to have particular problems. If you can invest some time in this early on in the course it may save you time later.
- Carry out a simple, written survey of the class, asking which parts of the course they find most difficult and why. Collate the results and see if there are any patterns.
- Discuss the students' expectations of and approach to learning with them. Find out what they think the course is really about, what it asks of them. Do they see it in terms of deep or surface learning? How do they approach it? What strategies do they use to cope with it? It is probably best to do this spontaneously on the back of other topics rather than try to address it directly.
- If you have some control over the scheme of work, do not try to cover so much in a single session. Allow more time for question and answer and checking understanding. However, if the course is set, you will have to condense some other (hopefully easier) topic.
- Make sure the assessment questions are consistent with the kind of learning you want to encourage. Whatever you say about the course, the students will take their cue from these. Pay particular attention to the verbs used in questions, such as *name, list, describe, compare, apply, use, explain, consider, examine, evaluate*. . . Do they call for memorization and reproduction or for more complex forms of analysis, understanding, application or evaluation? (See Notes.)

Make a note below of any of these solutions that you could adopt or any others that come to mind.

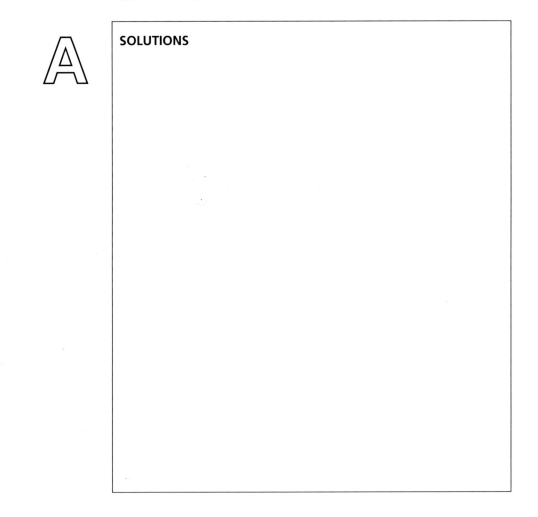

A

SOLUTIONS

5 ARE THE LEARNING TASKS APPROPRIATE?

NO ☐   ? ☐   YES ☐

Tasks, exercises and activities are central to teaching and learning. Some of these tasks are collective and involve a whole class or subgroup, others are individual. Some will take place during the session; others will be for afterwards, in the form of homework or private study. The nature of tasks varies greatly, reflecting the content of the subject, the level of study and the overall aims of the course. Sometimes such tasks will be formally assessed and marked, sometimes not. But their purpose is always the same, which is to engage the student in active learning, to involve him or her in actually *doing* the subject.

- What kinds of task do you give the students during the class?
- What kinds of task do you set them outside the class?
- Can you choose the tasks or are they built into the course?
- Do the students have any say in deciding on the tasks?
- Do the students understand the specification (as distinct from the content) of the tasks? Do they ask about this?
- Do they understand why these particular tasks are useful?
- Could you reduce the time they spend on tasks without affecting their learning?

Learning can usefully be seen in terms of tasks because it is an activity, something we do. It implies some kind of engagement with the world, and it is this that distinguishes it from the more passive forms of entertainment or leisure. Indeed, tasks can be regarded as a kind of intensified experience, doing in a concentrated way something that outside the course environment might be spread over a much longer period of time.

There is a wide range of possible tasks, reflecting both the type of learning and the nature of the subject involved. The simplest tasks require the straightforward rehearsal or *reproduction* of what is being learned, as in rote or descriptive learning or the practice of skills. However, most learning tasks at the post-compulsory stage go beyond this and require the student to *do something with the information*: add to it, select from it, modify it, respond to it, compare it, extrapolate it, manipulate it, substitute for it, translate it, apply it or otherwise use or deploy it in some way.

The most demanding tasks, however, involve not simply reproduction or manipulation but *re-construction*, so that the student has to process the information or input in highly complex ways, by analysing, interpreting, synthesizing, designing, re-creating, evaluating or somehow reconstituting it in theory or practice. Some tasks are set specifically to develop the capacity to *transfer* a learned process from one situation to another. Most courses involve a range of tasks, combining various elements of the above.

One problem with learning tasks is simply their familiarity. Each subject and type of education has its typical, well-established and sometimes hallowed repertoire of classroom and homework tasks: drills, exercises, presentations, essays, experiments, reports, projects and so on. We need to stand back from these and ask: What are they for? Exactly how do they promote learning? For example, it is widely assumed that arts students have to write a lot of essays, and science students spend a lot of time in the lab. But why?

We also need to be wary of activity for activity's sake. It is easy to set a group some task simply to keep them occupied and give the appearance of learning. But in fact they may be going over old ground again, or doing something that does not contribute directly to their learning. Tasks have to be chosen in the light of objectives, not just because they seem like work (or fun).

Another problem arises when there is insufficient guidance about the task. Do the students know what they are meant to do and how they should go about it? More than that: can they see the point of the task, or is it just some meaningless hoop they have to jump through? If so, they will do just that.

Tasks also need to be aligned with assessment. They should reflect the criteria and mirror the process by which the students' performance will be judged. It is not fair to students to get them used to one kind of task or activity in the class and then assess them in a quite different way, unless one is deliberately testing that kind of transfer.

In some practical or applied fields, 'real-life' tasks may have an obvious attraction in terms of immersing the students in the authentic situation. However, mere exposure or experience is not enough in itself to ensure learning; there has to be careful briefing, debriefing and reflection to get the best out of it.

Finally, there may be simpler practical problems. Students may not be given enough time to complete the task properly before being hurried on to the next one. Judging how long tasks take in class is quite an art, and can vary from group to group; experienced teachers seem to develop antennae coming out of their heads for this. Students may not be given adequate notice of assignments. Or they may not have access to the resources or materials they need at the time they need them. Several major tasks or assignments may coincide at the same time, creating problems of bunching and priority. Learning tasks need to be manageable to be useful.

WHAT'S THE PROBLEM?

Here are some solutions to think about:

- Look carefully at your course materials to make sure that the guidance on tasks is detailed enough. However, where working out the nature of the task is part of the task, be careful not to spoon-feed students.
- When you brief students about a task in the class, double-check that they really understand. Do not rush them; deal patiently with their queries. If you think they are too inhibited to ask individually, organize them in small groups for the briefing and give them a few minutes to discuss it before asking questions.
- When you get students' work, check it for any signs of common or persistent misinterpretation of the task specification.

- If you give students a task to complete in the class, either check how much longer they need to finish or give them a few minutes' warning: don't halt the activity abruptly.
- List the kinds of tasks you set and ask yourself systematically of each one: How does this actually promote learning? Is it really necessary?
- Discuss with your subject colleagues the kinds of tasks that are usually set and whether these are justified by something more than habit and precedent. Invite a colleague or two from other subjects; outsiders may question your habits or assumptions.
- Find out about the kinds of tasks set in different subjects or fields and see if any of them might be usable in your own. Build in a bit of variety. Surprise the students occasionally to keep them on their toes. Learning tasks can become boringly routine.
- Consider whether a task is best done individually or with other students. What do the students learn from either experience? You can vary even common tasks by changing this aspect of them.
- Check the congruence of the tasks you set with the way students are assessed. If the two are very different, change one or the other to bring them into line.

A

SOLUTIONS

This section on *tasks* and the next one on *feedback* are closely related and should be taken together.

6 DO THE STUDENTS GET ENOUGH FEEDBACK?

NO ☐   ? ☐   YES ☐

Feedback gives us information about the results or consequences of what we do and is as crucial in teaching and learning as in any other activity, forming part of the loop or cycle of self-regulation. The concept comes from the field of 'cybernetics', a term derived from the Greek word 'to steer', and that is precisely its function: it enables us to stay on course so that we eventually reach our chosen destination. Most feedback in teaching is verbal (either oral or written), though non-verbal hints and body language may also provide some signals. Students receive their main feedback from teachers but also get some from other students or people outside the situation, such as parents or colleagues. Feedback can relate to everything from one's informal participation in the group through work on classroom tasks and course assignments (Section 5) to performance in exams and assessment (see Sections 23 and 24). While students can do many things for themselves, feedback is one thing they usually need to get from someone else.

- Do students keep repeating mistakes, keep asking the same kinds of questions?
- Are there other signs of 'feedback deficiency'?
- Have you got enough time to give feedback during the class?
- Does the size of the class make it difficult to give individual feedback?
- Are you able to make enough comments on written work?
- Do the students take the feedback on board?
- Are they getting conflicting feedback from different sources?
- Do they get feedback but not until it is too late to do anything with it?

Feedback happens mainly through:

- teachers' comments on individuals' performance on tasks during the class;

- working together in a practical setting such as a workshop, laboratory or field trip;
- marks and written comments on homework and assignments;
- individual or small-group tutoring or supervision;
- marks and comments on assessed work and exams.

All but the last are formative: in other words, they allow students to shape their work as they are progressing. Feedback on assessed work is summative in the sense that it represents a final judgement, although it may contain lessons for the next course. Feedback and assessment are not the same; the purpose of the first is to improve learning, while the aim of the second is to evaluate it. It is crucial therefore to ask what opportunities students have to try out, and if necessary modify, what they do before they are finally assessed.

Timing may also be important. Rapid feedback is most important in skill learning, where unless an error is quickly corrected it can become embedded in practice and difficult to unlearn. With other kinds of learning, feedback need not be immediate but it should not be too long delayed, otherwise the learners will have forgotten what they did in the first place or have moved on to something else. There is also a balance to be struck between giving too little and too much feedback. The usual problem is too little, but if we want learners to develop and internalize the capacity to evaluate their own work – important in many jobs and the rest of life – we should encourage them to try judging it for themselves.

Most teachers are aware of the importance of feedback, at least in principle. In practice they may be too preoccupied with putting things across (*input*) to give enough. Some feedback is too vague or general to be of use; comments need to be quite detailed and specific to be informative. Staff workload and student numbers may reduce both classroom responses and written comments to a minimum. Good feedback should not only give a judgement on performance but also suggest ways of improving it, and this can be quite time consuming since the prescription may differ from case to case.

There is also an affective side to feedback: teachers need to be ready to give it and learners to receive it. Since some of it may be negative they may both be loath to do so. It has to be fine-tuned to suit the individual case: the same comment may bounce off one student but deeply wound another. Hence the typical advice to begin with something positive, but equally students will smell out insincere feedback very quickly; bland praise is worse than useless. It is also easy to slip into the bad habit of only commenting in order to correct things: students need regular, positive confirmation that what they are doing is good or on the right track.

The style of feedback depends not just on the individual teacher but on the wider educational and even social culture. It may range from 'tough-minded' to 'tender-hearted'. Some courses and teachers pride themselves on being the former, on the grounds that it is a necessary part of the education or training: medicine is a prime example. It is useful to reflect on the prevailing ethos in your field and the extent to which you are comfortable with it.

As noted at the beginning, this is perhaps the one function of teaching that learners find most difficult to internalize and do for themselves. Even research students look to their supervisors to critique their theses. That said, the capacity to do good work and the capacity to judge that work are closely intertwined and we should try to develop the process of self-regulation and 'inner feedback' wherever possible.

WHAT'S THE PROBLEM?

Consider the following solutions:

- When you are asking or answering questions make sure you are satisfied with the outcome of the dialogue; if necessary, pursue it a little further in the class or talk to the student at the end of it.

- You may need to move towards a more interactive style of teaching, working through question and answer, and spending more time on dialogue and discussion. However, this may mean that the students will have to get much of the input (see Section 3) on their own. You need to be sure they are capable of doing this and ready to take increased responsibility for their own learning.
- If you have time, hold 'surgeries' where students can discuss their work problems with you on a one-to-one basis.
- Prepare a standard *pro forma* that lists common feedback comments on written work and tick the relevant ones in each case; but add some individual comments as well, otherwise it will seem too impersonal.
- Exchange assignments with a colleague to see what kinds of written feedback you both give.
- Change the overall design of the course to ensure that there are enough opportunities for formative feedback as distinct from summative assessment.
- Video one of your own classes to see what kind of low-level, running feedback you give to students. What tacit, affective messages does it send? What do the students pick up from it? Has your style changed over time? If so, why? Imagine what it is like to be on the receiving end.

Make notes below on possible solutions to feedback problems.

| SOLUTIONS |
| |

You have now completed the six cognitive functions and this may be a good point to pause and perhaps fill in part of the profile summary at the end of the chapter (page 66), referring back to each section as you do so to double check your response. You will begin to get a sense of the pattern of your teaching and where the problems (if any) lie.

The next three functions relate to the affective or emotional side of classroom work. These may be more difficult to pin down in terms of specific incidents or events; as noted earlier, they are often a matter of the general atmosphere or tone of the class and the relationship between teacher and student. That does not mean that they are any less important; indeed for some in the post-compulsory field, and in particular further education, they may represent the main challenge.

7 ARE THE STUDENTS MOTIVATED TO LEARN?

NO ☐   ? ☐   YES ☐

Learning always has to compete with other needs, demands and interests. Even at the level of moment-to-moment attention, it is always subject to loss of concentration or distraction. The mind can wander. The time students spend in class could be spent doing other things, or nothing. And there are always 'opportunity costs' involved in following a course, which mean that people cannot devote that time and energy to other activities or relationships. Motivation is the word we use to describe the fact that, for whatever reason, people prioritize learning on all these different levels. If they do not, it shows up as lack of attention or concentration, lack of effort or commitment, lack of persistence or 'stickability'. Are any of these a problem in your class?

- Do the students turn up? Do they attend regularly?
- Do any of them disrupt the class and cause discipline problems?
- Do they pay attention? Do they concentrate on the tasks they are given?
- Do they do the preparatory and follow-up work? Do they do the reading?
- Is lack of motivation associated with particular topics?
- Is it associated with particular stages in the course?
- Do the students become demotivated after a promising start?
- Do you understand their motivation or lack of it?
- Do you know why they are on the course?

The very word motivation suggests a kind of energy that propels us through the learning process. However, it is better seen as a matter of preferences and choices that operate at a number of levels. For example, even 'well motivated' students may still find it hard to concentrate on a classroom task or reading assignment, because their minds are preoccupied with something else. Another student may have a laser-like focus on what he or she is doing at the time but not be especially interested in that particular class. Others again may be disciplined and hard-working without feeling involved in the subject. The question to ask in each case is: what competes for time and attention? What are the alternatives? What other thoughts, activities or fantasies does the learner prefer?

Theories of motivation tend to stress either internal factors (such as drives, curiosity and need for achievement) or external factors such as reward, belonging, status and reinforcement (see Notes). In practice, there is often a mixture that may itself change over time. A student might enrol on a course because friends have done so (social motivation), continue with it because the subject turns out to be interesting (intrinsic motivation), and complete it because it leads to a job (extrinsic motivation). Students may want to prove something to themselves (personal motivation). Peer pressure can be important and role models (or lack of them) may also be significant.

One of the general issues is the extent to which motivation is attributed to or seen as the responsibility of the teacher or student (see Appendix 2). At a minimum, teachers will usually agree that they should avoid demotivating students through poor teaching or by completely ignoring their needs and interests. However, once we get beyond the end of compulsory schooling, students on most courses are there on a voluntary (if sometimes pressurized) basis and must therefore take some of the responsibility for their own motivation. Having said that, most students experience ups and downs on their courses, and it is during the latter that the teacher can play a key role in encouraging them to stay with it.

The origins of motivation go well beyond the classroom or course and reach deep into the family or community (see Section 22). Although you may think of your students as individuals, they form part of a much wider economic and social setting that has its own prevailing attitudes and values. There may be social class or subcultural differences in terms of how they, their parents, their peers or their employers view education and academic achievement. Alienation from the system is a particular problem in some inner-city areas. Some employers (still) think training is a waste of time. Overseas students bring values from their home cultures. Are you aware of such differences within the groups you teach? And are you aware of them in yourself?

Practical issues may also affect motivation. Many students now work part-time to fund themselves, and beyond a certain point this can cut into the time and effort they devote to their courses. People who study at a distance through 'open learning' can feel isolated. Those attending classes in the evening may be tired after a long day. Age eventually takes its toll in terms of energy and attention.

Note down the main issues below. Since motivation (or lack of it) is sometimes a difficult thing to interpret, it may be particularly useful to talk this one over with colleagues first.

WHAT'S THE PROBLEM?

Since motivation often reflects wider influences and circumstances, we can't always do much about it. However, here are some ideas to think about:

- If lack of attention or concentration is a problem, build some variety into the session. Break up your talk with short activities that require the students to respond. Use a range of visual or verbal inputs. Involve different voices or contributors. This is particularly necessary in longer classes (eg, two hours or more).
- Attention can often dip in the middle of a longer activity, especially if it is a repetitive one such as a lecture or practice session. Build in some change – even just of pace or presentation – at that stage.
- Get a colleague to listen to your style of presentation in terms of pace, tone, delivery and energy, and see if you can make it more interesting. Use the room: walk around if that seems appropriate.
- A little humour goes a long way. The occasional anecdote can help. Try to lighten things up, establish a more human or personal contact with the group. After all, you are not just teachers and students, but people.
- Link what the class is doing at each point to the eventual out-comes: assignments, essays, exams and so on. Give students a sense of purpose.
- If there are routine or boring topics to get through, explain the point of them. Do not just treat them as given.
- Do not forget to say or write well done. Students, like all of us, need periodic encouragement, and this applies to the best as well as the weakest.
- Draw on social motivation. Allow the students to interact and enjoy working with one another in pairs or larger groups.
- If appropriate, draw on employment motivation. Even if some students are bored with the course, they may still want to com-plete it in order to try to get a job at the end. Arrange visits to workplaces to give them a taste of the likely fruits.
- If some students seem to be really alienated, talk to them indiv-idually or in a small group to try to find out why. (See also Sections 21 and 22.)
- Look carefully at the guidance that students get before they choose a course. Is it adequate? Is there any possibility of sampling courses, or switching if they realize they have made a mistake?
- If the lack of motivation seems to reflect the wider social or cultural context, try to involve the relevant third parties such as parents or employers in discussions about it. This may not be easy in the case of disaffected school-leavers and their families (see Section 22).

There is a good deal of overlap between this section on *motivation* and the next two on *belief* and *reward*. Although they can be read on their own, they are best treated as a cluster of related issues.

8 DO THE STUDENTS BELIEVE IN THEMSELVES?

NO ☐   ? ☐   YES ☐

Even if we are motivated to learn something, we may or may not believe that we can. That belief – or lack of it – may stem from past experiences, similar occasions when we either did or did not manage to achieve what we wanted. Or it may arise from the lack of a comparable experience that would give us some indication of whether we are likely to cope this time. Both of these cases underline the importance of the student's 'learning history' and the kind of self-concept or self-image that he or she may have developed as a result. Lack of self-belief can lead to students giving up when the going gets tough, or even prevent them embarking on a course or attempting a task in the first place. By contrast, a positive and realistic view of their own potential helps them sustain their learning during the course and in particular through any bad patches. Confidence is crucial.

- Do any of your students seem particularly lacking in confidence?
- How do you notice or pick up that lack of confidence? Do they seem shy in class? Unwilling to contribute? Uncertain about their assignments?
- Does the lack of confidence relate to specific topics or to the subject as a whole?
- What do they attribute that lack of confidence to? Do they say?
- What do you attribute it to?
- Do any students appear overconfident? If so, does that apparent confidence mask self-doubt in some cases?

Although teachers have long recognized, in a common-sense way, the need to build up students' confidence, the emphasis on learners' self-image and sense of self-efficacy are relatively modern themes in educational psychology, reflecting the growth of humanistic theories in particular and the concern with 'affect' (feelings) in general. The importance of the self-concept to students' behaviour and performance is now widely recognized and the phrase 'emotional intelligence' has recently entered the vocabulary as well (see Notes). Self-belief and self-efficacy can be seen as 'meta' aspects of learning in that they represent general views of oneself, but since they may also relate to specific tasks ('I'm hopeless at X. . .') or situations ('I don't belong in this class/course/place') they are related here to motivation (Section 7) and reward (Section 9).

By the time students get to the post-16 stage they already have a long learning history, which goes back not only through secondary and primary school but to the pre-school years that may be very important in terms of these issues. They are likely to have formed some picture of both the level and profile of their own abilities (how good I am/what I am good at) and the gap, if any, between what they are capable of and what they have actually achieved so far. This gap may involve factors such as family background (lack of support) the influence of particular teachers (he put me off maths) or schools (I hated it there). Certain individuals (relations, employers, older colleagues) may act as mentors then or later in life. So the teacher in further, higher or continuing education is coming in quite late in the story, and may encounter well-established beliefs and perceptions about the 'learner-self' that may be negative or positive.

Among these may be a tendency to attribute what happens to oneself (a sense of agency or responsibility) or to the world around one (a sense of things happening to one, of being on the receiving end). So attribution theory – the way we relate outcomes to causes – can help us explore the extent to which the student feels he or she is, or is not, in control (see Notes). This matters particularly in an institutional setting such as education, where less-confident individuals may feel daunted or oppressed by the weight of the system or the authority of the teacher.

The self-image, and the related locus of control, are also social or role constructs that emerge from the history and pattern of family, peer and work relationships. It can be difficult to disentangle the way the student presents himself or herself and communicates with and relates to others in the class from the set of beliefs that the person has about his or her own potential. Thus shyness in the class does not always indicate a lack of self-confidence about learning, and sometimes the difference between a student's oral (public) and written (private) performance can be quite striking.

Learning is sometimes a struggle and, as noted earlier, most students experience ups and downs that may become apparent from their behaviour and attitude in the class. The sensitive teacher will usually pick up such changes and try to offer some words of encouragement. Students may also give one another support to help a friend through a particular educational or personal problem or emotional trough. Lack of self-belief only turns into a serious issue when it actually inhibits people from embarking on education in the first place, or becomes a persistent or pervasive factor that undermines the very capacity to learn and (rather like depression) goes beyond the specific circumstances that might justify it. In the most serious cases, it requires professional help that goes beyond the remit of the ordinary teacher, and one of the things lecturers and teachers need to learn is when to refer students on for this.

WHAT'S THE PROBLEM?

Here are some strategies to consider:

- Begin with some easier tasks so that students can experience some success early on. That will help build up their confidence for the harder bits ahead.
- Likewise, do not hit them with something really difficult at the outset, unless this is a deliberate 'break them down, build them up' strategy that is justified in the circumstances.
- Break large tasks down into manageable chunks or small steps. Take one thing at a time.
- Make sure that students have really consolidated and mastered each stage or task, even if that takes a bit longer. Give them the feeling of competence, not just scraping through by the skin of their teeth. This will pay off gradually in terms of a growing sense of confidence and security.

- With individuals who generally lack self-belief and have a negative self-image, find something that they can do well and accentuate that. Build their confidence outwards from that core towards the more challenging tasks.
- Talk to students about their previous experience, their 'learning history'. Find out what has happened to shape their view of themselves as students. You will need to build up their trust to do this.
- Explore their perception of risk (of failing, looking a fool, letting themselves or other people down). There may have been 'critical incidents' in the past that have affected this. Again, you may need to get to know them quite well before you can do this.
- Create opportunities for them to support one another. Let them work together and draw on one another's strengths. Let each individual see how he or she can contribute particular skills to the overall task. Try to build a co-operative ethos through group presentations or projects.
- Use individual or small group tutorials to explore these more personal aspects of learning, though this is often best done spontaneously on the back of something else rather than by making an issue of them. These are sensitive topics and need to be approached with a sense of tact and timing.
- If the schedule allows, give students time. Often an informal, unplanned chat outside the class can mean a lot, simply because someone (for a change) has bothered in an otherwise indifferent world.

SOLUTIONS

9 DO THE STUDENTS FIND THEIR LEARNING REWARDING?

NO ☐   **?** ☐   **YES** ☐

Learning is in some ways a delicate, fragile, tenuous thing. It involves some kind of change in consciousness (what we know, how we think) or behaviour (what we do, how we act), but getting that change established in the first place can be difficult. It is not always easy to absorb new information, grasp new ideas, develop new strategies, master new skills. Even when we do learn something, we can lose it again. We have only to think of all the things we once knew or did at school that are now only dim, distant memories. Likewise we may once have acquired skills (in sports, crafts, arts) that have now become rusty. All this points to the need to consolidate or strengthen learning to ensure that it becomes well established in the first place and does not fade afterwards. Various things may be important in that process: practice is essential in the learning of skills, meaning in the development of understanding, awareness in the development of strategies. But if one had to pick out one general factor that affected all forms of learning it would probably be a sense of reward. This raises two basic questions:

- Do the students get satisfaction from their learning?
- Do they get rewarded for the work they do?

Behavioural psychologists in the first half of the twentieth century developed a whole theory of learning and reinforcement on the 'pain–pleasure' principle involving various forms of punishment and reward (see Notes). Much of their experimental work was carried out with animals and birds such as rats and pigeons. This has often since been derided for being simplistic, or criticized as a technique for manipulating behaviour, although people sometimes forget that it did help to bring about a major swing in contemporary educational practice away from reliance on various kinds of punishment (beatings, lines, detention, etc) to an emphasis on positive reinforcement (attention, praise, grades, etc).

Applying ideas of reward and punishment to human beings is a good deal more complex than with animals (some people, for example, find pain pleasurable), but the concept of reward remains a central one in learning and teaching as in the rest of human behaviour. It is important therefore to think about the kinds of reassurance, reward, pleasure or satisfaction the student gets, and about our role as teachers in helping to create this. To begin with, a student's initial enthusiasm can be eroded by a lack of any real pleasure or enjoyment in what he or she is doing. After all, learning is work (and often hard work), and as the management books say we all require some job satisfaction. Likewise, the absence of any positive reward or confirmation may gradually eat away at the student's sense of self-efficacy. We will return to the broader aspects of reward at the level of the course as a whole in Section 26, but here it is important to consider it in a more immediate way in the context of the session. At this level, three kinds of reward come into play.

The first is the *personal or inner reward* that the student may experience. He or she may get a sense of achievement in doing or completing something that was difficult or challenging, and that perhaps seemed out of reach at the beginning. The sense of meaning that comes from understanding or interpreting something can also be deeply satisfying. Likewise, it can be very rewarding to create or construct something new, whether that is a physical artefact, a work of art or a novel way of organizing a process. There may be satisfaction in a growing sense of competence or control, for example in a concrete skill or practical activity. There is also a basic feeling of reward, however elusive, in the sense that somehow one has moved forward or progressed.

Educational rewards come from the teacher, one's peers, the institution or the system. At the simplest level, these consist of attention, interest and praise in the class and the respect that one may get from others. There may be pleasure in the sheer doing of the subject and the interaction with one's friends. Beyond that, educational rewards take the more concrete forms of marks, grades, progression to higher levels and ultimately qualifications. Finally, outside the domain of education, there are the various, broader *socio-economic rewards* of esteem, security, acceptance, reputation, jobs and job satisfaction, relationships and – last but not least – money.

Some of these rewards are within the gift of the teacher; others lie well beyond the teacher's sphere. Individual students will need or look for some rewards rather than others. The person who experiences intense inner satisfaction in his or her work may not care about a teacher's approbation or a sense of belonging. Other students will rely heavily on the positive comments of the teacher or membership of the group. Others again will look beyond education altogether to job prospects or life chances. It may not matter too much what kind of rewards students have as long as they have some. The problem comes when there are, or they can see, none.

WHAT'S THE PROBLEM?

As noted above, some rewards for learning are either so personal and subjective or so broad and social that there may be little the teacher can do about them. However, depending on the type of learning involved and the kind of problem you have identified, you may want to think about some of the following strategies:

- Welcome students' contributions in class, even if they are not always apt or correct. Do not simply dismiss them. Avoid sarcasm. Do not put students down; they will remember this for years afterwards.
- Give praise for good work both orally and in writing. Listen to yourself in the class and watch what you write in terms of comments on students' work.
- Recognize honest effort and hard work, even if it is not always good. Acknowledge the learner even if the learning falls short.
- Find ways of rewarding the whole group if they do good work. Tell them that they have done well. Celebrate with them. Reward is not just an individual thing.
- Relate what the students are doing to their assessment and results. Make sure they see the link and understand the consequences of their attitude and actions.

- Demonstrate the intrinsic rewards of the subject by showing the pleasure you get from it. Enthusiasm rubs off; so does disillusion.
- If appropriate, refer to the potential longer-term social or economic rewards of learning in terms of getting a job, promotion, security, status and the like. But be realistic and honest about the prospects.
- Think carefully about how students are 'punished'. Just because we do not use the word much any more does not mean that punishment does not exist. Is it a matter of rejection by one's peers? Loss of esteem? Withdrawal of teacher interest or support? Institutional sanctions? Repeated failure? Exclusion?

A

SOLUTIONS

The two remaining sections in this chapter have to do with the 'meta' functions of *exploration* and *reflection*. If you need to, refer back to the teaching–learning triangle on page 14 to remind you of the overall structure.

10 DO THE STUDENTS EXPLORE WHAT THEY LEARN?

NO ☐   ? ☐   YES ☐

These last two sections in 'Trouble-shooting the session' have to do with exploration and reflection. The difference between them is that exploration points *outwards* towards what is being learned – the topic, content or subject matter – and reflection points *inwards* towards the learner and the process of learning. However, it can sometimes be difficult to separate the two, and indeed it does not matter too much if we cannot. They are both aspects of meta-cognition: knowing about knowing, thinking about thinking, learning about learning. The idea of exploration is best seen in relation to that of understanding (Section 4). Although understanding involves questions about what one is learning, exploration questions what one is learning. It treats the subject matter – its scope, nature, parameters, basis – as problematic. It does not take the content for granted but explores its substance, boundaries and methods. As such, it begins to dig up the very ground we are standing on.

- Do the students question the basis of what they are learning?
- Do they display a critical approach in class?
- Are they willing to explore tangents or related issues?
- Is discussion or dialogue an important part of the teaching?
- Does the assessment test critical thinking?
- Does the assessment allow for creative or original thinking?
- Is enquiry a general aim of the course?
- Is enquiry part of the culture of the institution?

Not all courses and teaching aim to develop critical or exploratory thinking and this is not necessarily a criticism; it all depends on what you are trying to do. For example, you might be teaching a one-off session or short course with quite limited objectives that leave no time or room for this kind of exploratory approach. You might be laying the 'building blocks' for what may later become a much more open-ended process. You may argue that students need to know something about the topic before they can begin to question its assumptions or probe its boundaries. You might concentrate on developing mastery of techniques before starting to talk about originality.

There may also be a deeper conflict between inducting students into a particular way of thinking and behaving and questioning that very thought and behaviour. Many professional training courses aim to develop a certain set of values and practices – think for example of nursing – but even in general education there may be limits to enquiry imposed both by the culture of the institution and the subculture of the discipline. Thus a secondary school might want to inculcate certain norms, and a historian or chemist certain ways of 'doing' the subject. In higher education, where the aim of critical thinking is generally proclaimed, one runs into the ultimate paradox of whether the idea of the 'critical' should not itself be subject to critical thinking. And to what extent is there a conflict between the critical and the creative at any level of work?

There are thus various issues to do with the whole idea of exploration and, as noted in the introduction to this chapter, it may not be one of your prime objectives. However, 'dialogue' and 'enquiry' form part of the general rhetoric of education and also increasingly of training, where they tend to have a more applied or utilitarian emphasis; brainstorming and problem solving are activities for a purpose, not ends in themselves.

The first question is whether exploration forms part of your agenda at all. If it does not and there are good reasons for this, you can move on. If it does, you may need to examine the relationship between what you say about exploration (in terms of stated aims and objectives) and what actually goes on in the classroom. If there is a gap between the two, the problem may lie in the previous experience and current expectations of the group (they simply want to get on with it), the kind of learning environment you create for them (which may be tightly structured), the kind of model you present to them (which may discourage spontaneity) and above all the ways you assess them (which may penalize risk taking).

Exploration also brings with it certain risks. At a minimum it can waste time; by its very nature, there is no guarantee that it will prove productive. You may also find it difficult to manage the discussion or get back on track. It might not be easy to distil what has come out of the process at the end. All these are worries that can make you (or the students) want to return to safer pastures. There is also a more general problem of insecurity. Learning itself involves change, which can be hazardous, and when it takes place in a public arena (such as the class) it can be quite threatening.

Questioning what you are actually doing adds another dimension of uncertainty for both you and the students. It may also stir up trouble with colleagues or bring you into conflict with the culture of the institution.

Having said all this, there remain powerful reasons for emphasizing this meta-cognitive function of teaching and learning. Life, at least in our society, seems to be becoming more open-ended, less certain. Roles are less stable. Identities are up for grabs. Age and gender no longer carry the expectations that they did. There may be no right way to solve a problem, no single interpretation of a text or event, no general consensus about the best approach, no canonical practice. Received wisdom and accepted authority seem to count for less than they did. We may not like these changes but they have implications for the way we prepare people for, and help them to live in, this world.

WHAT'S THE PROBLEM?

Here are some ideas to try:

- Give yourself and your students more space. Cut down on the amount you cover, or use independent study materials to cover it, if that is practicable.
- Do not worry too much about going off on tangents if they seem interesting or fruitful, but devise ways of getting back to the main script again when you need to.
- Encourage the unusual and difficult questions. There will usually be someone in the group who can bring an unconventional angle

to the discussion. You may not appreciate their awkwardness but the challenge can be valuable.

● Have a 'Plan B' that you can revert to if your high-risk methods do not seem to be working.

● Think hard about the model or example you set. What messages do the students get from your approach? Are you syllabus-bound or syllabus-free? Do you open things up or close them down?

● Discuss your and the students' expectations of the course with them. They may not engage in exploratory learning because they are not used to it or because they don't realize that you expect it.

● Use methods that encourage exploratory work, such as brainstorming, scenario-building, role plays, debates, projects. But set out the ground rules clearly, especially the first time, so that the students know where they are.

● Talk to students about the course outside the course. They may open up over a cup of coffee where they wouldn't in the more formal environment of the classroom.

● Look carefully at the assessment methods and questions to see what kind of learning they embody. If necessary, and if you can, change them to allow for more open-ended, speculative or creative thinking.

SOLUTIONS

11 DO THE STUDENTS REFLECT ON THEIR LEARNING?

NO ☐   ? ☐   YES ☐

The second meta-cognitive function is reflection: awareness of the process of learning. Reflection is a key element in all forms of practice; it involves standing back and having a good look at the way we do things. Without such reflection, we are prone to sink into mindless habit and unthinking routine, with all the inherited assumptions and habitual baggage we have picked up along the way. Moreover, there is little chance that we will actually learn from our mistakes and develop new approaches. Learning is no different from any other form of practice. Students bring to it a bundle of habits, techniques and assumptions that they have put together from their previous experience, good or bad. By the time they get to the post-compulsory stage, those habits may have become firmly entrenched, even unconscious. (How many people think about the way they read?) But the need for reflection does not arise simply from the continuity of old practices. It stems from the change in demands on the student that post-compulsory education makes. This is particularly true of transitions from one sector (eg, school) to another (FE, HE) where the whole ethos and pattern of study may be different. It can also apply to the progression from one year or stage to the next. Above all, these changes relate to assessment and the different criteria and methods that may be involved. For all these reasons, learning at the post-school stage really needs to happen on two levels: learning, and learning about learning.

- Do the students seem comfortable with the style of work?
- Do they seem uncertain about how to approach parts of the work?
- Are you sometimes surprised by the way they approach it?
- Do they sometimes misinterpret the nature of the task?
- Are they aware of their own style of learning?
- Can they work independently?

A good deal of education is rather unreflective. Students simply get on with their work, making their way through the course as best they can, from one week or month to the next. The pressures of the curriculum mean that both teachers and students often feel there is little time to stand back and reflect on how it is going. The introduction of AS levels, for example, has meant that there is no let-up now in assessment for those in the 16–18 age bracket, and modularization in higher education has much the same effect (though it has some advantages too).

As long as things are progressing reasonably well, staff may prefer not to open up a can of worms to do with the process of learning, although they will usually attend to individual difficulties. In the hard-headed training world there may be even less tolerance of what is regarded as navel-gazing, and in education such reflection and questioning is sometimes seen as undermining the teacher's and institution's authority.

There are three reasons, however, why we should reflect regularly on learning. The first is that it is part of the broader concept of education, which implies not simply knowing things but a degree of consciousness about that knowledge and the process that leads to it. Without reflection, education can slip into mere indoctrination or socialization. Second, learning is usually more effective if people can think about the strategies, styles, tactics and skills they use. Of course one may be aware of a bad habit or ineffective approach without necessarily being able to change it; after all, we are talking about what are often deeply ingrained practices. Third, one of the most important transferable skills that people can develop is precisely that of learning. This may be regarded as a mere spin-off from the learning of something, but we need to take more deliberate steps to develop it. The capacity to transfer and apply learning skills and strategies in different contexts depends partly on the degree of 'executive' knowledge and control we have over it (see Notes). The management of learning has to go right up to the managing director, as it were.

As noted in the introduction to this chapter, reflection (like exploration) has an affective aspect, and that can also act as a barrier to it. We may not be comfortable with the idea. It may expose poor habits or weaknesses, or call our self-image into question. It may not form part of the ethos of our subject, especially if that values objectivity and impersonality. We may not know how to do it. Where do we begin? What should we reflect on? What counts as good reflection? Which all goes to say that, while reflection is a good idea, it does not happen easily or naturally in practice and as teachers we need to find ways to encourage and facilitate it.

WHAT'S THE PROBLEM?

Here are some means of helping students to reflect on their own learning processes:

- When learning issues arise naturally during the class, take time to explore them, even at the expense of covering the ground. This is probably better than setting aside planned occasions for such discussions. The latter can seem artificial, though they may work.
- Be continually on the lookout for problems of approach, tactics and skills in the work you see. If these seem widespread, take time out to address them with the whole group.
- Make time to deal with acute, individual problems. Recognize that to the person concerned such problems may well seem urgent by the time they are brought to you.
- Give students sample pieces of work to mark in small groups. This will help tease out their implicit ideas about what is good or appropriate in terms of learning.
- Ask them to write short accounts of good and bad learning experiences in the past, and then discuss these in small groups. Draw out any general lessons from them.
- Get them to keep a diary over a period of weeks or months. This is a major exercise but can yield great benefits. They should have complete control over which parts of this they share with you or others.

- Explore how they manage their learning with them (see Notes).
- Action learning, which involves learning from what one is doing in a job or elsewhere, can be a powerful vehicle for reflection, though it is obviously limited to certain subjects and courses.
- Show that you reflect on your own teaching. If you feel you can, disclose your choices and uncertainties to the students. Say when you think something did not work well. Bring them in on the process.
- As always, look at the criteria and methods of assessment. Do these promote or inhibit reflection? What kinds of words do the assessors use to praise or criticize the work? These will give you some idea of the relative value placed on reflectivity.

SOLUTIONS

Anything else?

We have now analysed the 11 teaching functions, but before going on to fill in the profile summary you should consider whether there are any other aspects of your classroom work that you want to explore. The previous sections should have covered the main elements of your teaching sessions, but individual classes, teachers and situations vary a great deal and there may be something else that you need to trouble-shoot. If so, make notes on it below.

WHAT'S THE PROBLEM?

Now consider the range of possible solutions in the usual way.

SOLUTIONS

Please turn now to the profile and action plan that will draw together your findings for this chapter.

Profile

Now that you have completed Chapter 1, look back through your responses to each section and complete the profile below. You can revise your initial response if that now seems appropriate. The profile will give you a general picture of your teaching sessions and any problems you have identified. Ring each response as follows: NO = 1 or 2; ? = 3, 4 or 5; YES = 6 or 7. Use your own judgement in transposing your original three-point response onto this seven-point scale.

	No	?	Yes
1. Does your teaching build on the students' previous learning?	1 2 3 4 5 6 7		
2. Do the students know where they are going?	1 2 3 4 5 6 7		
3. Are the students getting the inputs they need?	1 2 3 4 5 6 7		
4. Do the students understand what they are learning?	1 2 3 4 5 6 7		
5. Are the learning tasks appropriate?	1 2 3 4 5 6 7		
6. Do the students get enough feedback?	1 2 3 4 5 6 7		
7. Are the students motivated to learn?	1 2 3 4 5 6 7		
8. Do the students believe in themselves?	1 2 3 4 5 6 7		
9. Do the students find their learning rewarding?	1 2 3 4 5 6 7		
10. Do the students explore what they learn?	1 2 3 4 5 6 7		
11. Do the students reflect on their learning?	1 2 3 4 5 6 7		
Anything else?	1 2 3 4 5 6 7		

Now turn to the next page and complete the action plan in the light of this.

Action plan

Note down the main actions you plan to take in connection with the problems you have identified. This will be a useful checklist that you can refer back to later as necessary, or discuss with your colleagues if you are working in a group. In each case, list the aim, the action (broken down into specific elements or stages if necessary), the person or persons responsible (including yourself) and the deadline(s).

AIM	ACTION	PERSON	DEADLINE

2 Trouble-shooting the course

Introduction

Chapter 1 focused on what happens in the class or session. In this chapter, we look at the larger canvas of the course as a whole. By 'course' here is meant a self-contained piece of curriculum, such as a unit or module, which is complete in itself even though it may form part of a wider programme. Such a course will typically comprise a series of sessions, perhaps of various kinds, over a period of time that will often last for a term or semester but may extend over anything from a weekend to an academic year.

The questions in Chapter 1 do not disappear but become subsumed in a wider framework that is concerned not only with what goes on within a session but everything that bears on this: the initial selection and induct-ion of students, the resources they get, the structures they have, the support they receive, the environment they experience and, last but not least, the criteria and methods of assessment. The two final sections deal with the results of the course and the quality of experience it provides for both students and staff. By the end of the chapter you should have built up a general picture of your teaching at the level of the course or module and this should help place your analysis in Chapter 1 in a broader context.

The variety of post-compulsory education becomes much more evident at this level. While the basic processes of classroom teaching provide some common ground for those working in the various sectors, once one starts looking at entire courses marked differences begin to appear. Some of these relate to the structure or pattern of the curriculum, others to assessment and the role of awarding or accrediting bodies such as exam boards and professions. Different regulatory frameworks in further, higher and adult education mean that the amount of control teachers have over their work varies a great deal, and the culture of different kinds of institutions – school sixth forms, tertiary or further education colleges, universities, adult education services – can affect courses in all sorts of ways. The diversity of courses and qualifications is most marked at the 16–19 stage, where students may be following an academic (AS/A level) track, a technical track (BTEC/EDEXCEL/GNVQ/Vocational A Level) or a vocational track (NVQ, City and Guilds, RSA, LCC, etc). As you work through the chapter, it may be useful for you to look back at Figure 0.1 in the Introduction to reflect again on the kind of organization you work in and the extent to which your teaching is internally or externally controlled.

Working through the chapter

As with Chapter 1, you should choose one particular course to focus on and respond to each section in terms of that. This will give you a more concrete, realistic basis for analysis than if you try to generalize about your work. Most people will be teaching several courses at a time, and if yours vary a great deal you can go through the chapter a second time using a contrasting course and comparing the two profiles at the end. If necessary, use your own notepad to do this. If you are working through the chapter in a group, you will probably find that this throws up considerable diversity of experience anyway.

As you progress through this chapter, you will see that there are increasing links and overlaps between sections and the issues they raise. This is as it should be and will help you to build up a more integrated, organic view of your teaching. Some cross-references to other sections are suggested in the text, but feel free to move around it in any way you want; there is no fixed order here. You should follow the same sequence of steps (refer back to pages 4–5 in the Introduction if necessary) in working through each section, but with one added stage. Before you decide on your solutions, run them past the following checklist:

- *Cost:* How much will it cost? What kinds of costs will it entail? Will there be running costs as well as an initial investment? Can the cost be met from existing budgets or will it require extra spending? Can you tap additional funding?
- *Organization:* Will it require changes in procedures, processes or structures? Does it fall within current regulations? What impact will it have on the way people work? On the institution as a whole?

- *Staff:* How will it affect staff roles or relationships? Will it create extra work? Who will be involved? How might colleagues react to the idea? Will they or you need additional skills?
- *Time:* How much time will it take? How will that time be found? Who will find it? Is there a time limit to the commitment?
- *Assessment:* Will it affect the assessment of students? Will it change the assessment criteria or methods? Could there be problems with regulations or procedures?
- *Students:* What impact will it have on the students? Do you need to negotiate it with them? How are they likely to react? What will they gain from it?

Together these headings add up to the acronym COSTAS. Not all will be equally important in every case, but it is useful to get into the habit of checking any ideas you propose against them. Changes at the level of the course often have knock-on effects on other aspects of the work, and it is important that you think these through before other people do.

12 ARE THE STUDENTS ON THE RIGHT COURSE?

NO ☐ ? ☐ YES ☐

There are two sides to this question. Is the course right for the students? And are the students right for the course? Either way, we are talking about the appropriate match between them. If the two are not well matched, it can create all sorts of problems – not least of motivation – that even the best planning and teaching may not overcome. There are various facets to the match. The most basic is that of intention: are the aims of the course reasonably congruent with the personal goals of the learners? They do not have to be exactly the same, but there needs to be enough overlap to satisfy both parties. Even if they do coincide, there may be other kinds of mismatch. The content may not be quite what the learners expected, the course may be pitched at the wrong level for them, the style of teaching and learning may seem alien. They may not feel at home in the group or comfortable in the institution. The course may simply be at the wrong time or in the wrong place for them. It is important to tease out any such problems to see what can be done about them this time or next time round.

- Do the students sometimes seem bored or disaffected?
- Do some of them drop out quickly? If so, do they go to another course/institution? Can you find out?
- Do you sense that they have a different agenda?
- Do any of them openly say that they do not want to be there?
- Do they find the course too difficult or too easy?
- Are they surprised at the direction the course has taken?
- Are they comfortable with this style or type of work?
- Do they encounter any practical difficulties in attending?
- Do you get enough students in the first place?

First, we need to distinguish between a basic mismatch of this sort and the initial settling down period. It can take students a while to adapt to the new subject and pattern of study, not to mention you and the others in the group. The situation can represent a considerable jump or transition for them, and there may also be teething troubles with the course itself, particularly as the group sorts itself out. So if it is still early days, lend a sympathetic ear to the problem, but give it time.

However, even at the beginning you may sense that something is seriously wrong: that a particular student seems like a fish out of water, for example, or is quickly realizing that the subject is not what he or she came for. This can be quite difficult to pick up in a large group, particularly because such students may in fact hide their anxieties. It is important to explore any such problems as soon as you can, for example through a private chat at the end of the class. An early short test or assignment will often flush out potential mismatches. A serious mismatch is no fun for either student or teacher and there may be alternative courses or options available at that initial stage.

Why has the mismatch occurred at all? No recruitment or selection process is foolproof, and there are always going to be a few people who end up on the 'wrong' course for one reason or another. To begin with, there are various wider factors affecting the decision, ranging from parental, peer or employer pressure on the one hand to institutional pressures to meet recruitment targets on the other. Teachers themselves often have more influence on such choices than they realize, and students can find it difficult to dissociate a subject from the person who taught it. The pre-course information and guidance may or may not be adequate: the brochures might be glossy, but who answers the phone? And how good is the student grapevine? There may also be selection procedures based on previous results, interviews, entry tests and references. Most forms of educational assessment are better as retrospective than predictive measures, despite being often used as the latter.

We also have to face the fact that the 16+ years are often ones of *multiple* change for young people, and some simply do not know what they want. One option is to continue up the escalator (if there is one). Another is to try things out. So we should not always blame ourselves, our institutions or the would-be student for mismatches or dropouts. While these seem wasteful in the short term, they can with hindsight prove to have helped the person make the right educational or life choices in the end.

Unless there is a systemic problem of access, selection or progression to your course, mismatches are likely to be confined to a minority of students. The nature of the difficulties may well vary from person to person and have to be dealt with individually, which takes time and often involves liaising with other people and departments. Good advice can be as valuable to a student as good teaching, and most staff see this as part of their broader, pastoral role. However, at the post-16 stage some of the responsibility also lies with the student. There is a limit to what you can do.

If you are not attracting enough students onto your course in the first place you will need to look closely at your publicity and the processes by which they come to enrol. If you are operating in a competitive educational market, which is the case with most post-compulsory courses these days, you also need to be aware of what your competitors are doing. However, the problem may go deeper. You may not be offering what people want at all, in which case you have to look hard at the nature and content of the course (whether it is a whole programme or a module within it) and whether it meets current demand. And demand changes over time.

Note down any problems below.

> **WHAT'S THE PROBLEM?**

As with some of the other sections in this chapter, your ability to do anything about these problems may depend on your position in the institution, and some of the ideas below imply a degree of seniority and responsibility, at departmental or even institutional level. Even if your own role is limited, however, you can think about and perhaps argue for such changes. People at the 'chalkface' often have a better sense of what is going on than those further away from it.

- Build better connections with those who influence course choices, such as parents, previous or linked institutions, employers, advisers.
- Check the pre-course literature and revise it if necessary. Monitor the speed and quality of telephone and written responses to enrolment enquiries. Remember that the best marketing involves not just selling but building a good and continuing relationship with the customer.
- Hold open days, especially if people are not familiar with the campus or venue. They will want to get a feel for the place as well as the course. If appropriate, offer an opportunity for parents to become involved as well.
- Provide short 'taster' courses that students can sample before making their choice. This can also be done within programmes where there is an optional or modular system.
- Allow students to change course within a limited period of time: long enough for them to get a feel for the course, not so long as to make it impossible to start a different one. Monitor the pattern of and reasons for such changes since they may have implications for selection procedures or course design.
- Discuss the nature of the course with the students at the beginning. Make clear your expectations and explore theirs. Establish or negotiate some ground rules about the nature and style of work: a kind of informal contract.
- If there are options or pathways later in the course or programme, explain them to the students so that they can see what the possibilities are. This might influence their overall view of the course and make them readier to accept initial, compulsory parts or topics they do not like.
- Find out what alternatives to your course exist so that you can point students towards them if necessary. Build links with the advisory and careers services; these are sometimes under-used.
- If appropriate, consult potential students or end-users about the design of the course before you plan it and put it on. In the case of professional bodies, you may have to do this anyway in order to get accreditation.
- Make use of final course evaluations to find out about the initial match between students and courses.
- Many problems in the training field occur before and after rather than during training. Try to build up a triangular relationship between trainer, trainee and line manager. This will help not only

to ensure that the right trainees get sent on your courses, but that they are given the chance to use or apply what they have learned when they get back.

Note down below any solutions to the problems you have identified, bearing in mind the COSTAS checklist: cost, organization, staff, time, assessment, students.

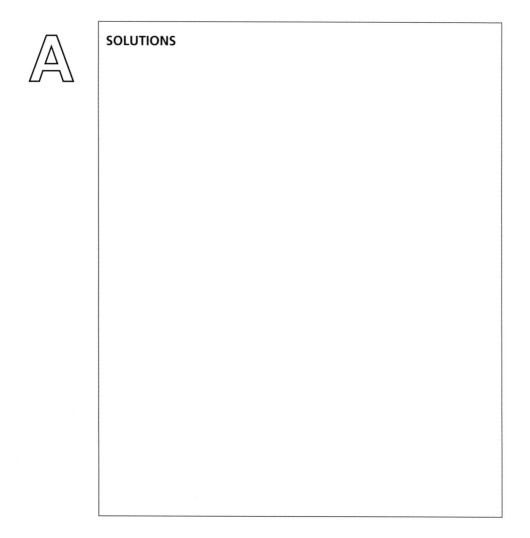

SOLUTIONS

13 DO THEY KNOW WHAT TO EXPECT?

NO ☐   ? ☐   YES ☐

Beginning a new course is often an embarkation into the unknown. The content is likely to be new. Not only that, the teacher may be a complete stranger and it could be the first time that the group has got together. Then there are the subtler uncertainties that students face. What can I expect? What is expected of me? How should I behave/dress/talk? What will the others be like? Will I fit in? What ground rules are there to do with work, interaction, communication? And (last but not least) what about the assessment? All these aspects of a new course create the need for some kind of induction or introduction that addresses at least some of these questions. And that need recurs to a lesser degree whenever there is a substantial new stage or branch in the programme, from level to level or year to year.

- Do the students seem hesitant or unsure at the beginning?
- Do they ask questions about where the course is going?
- Do they misunderstand some of the requirements or procedures?
- Do they seem confused or lost?
- What initial uncertainties come to light later?
- Do some seem to lose their way later on?
- Are they still asking 'basic' questions near the end of the course?

A course is a complex entity, involving structures, procedures, time frames, tasks, materials, relationships and outcomes. It is as complex as most jobs, and we would not usually throw someone in at the deep end of a new job without some kind of guidance. Some students, like some employees, seem to pick up cues and 'suss out' the situation more quickly than others, but most people need some kind of initial help to make sense of the environment they are entering. Otherwise they can spend a lot of time and energy at the beginning simply trying to find out what is going on and where they fit in. That can involve a steep learning curve, and one that distracts them from the real learning they are meant to be doing. It can also generate needless anxiety, loss of confidence and even a sense of being 'de-skilled'; suddenly, one's previous experience, know-how or expertise seem to count for little.

The problem is exacerbated by the fact that a good deal of teaching and learning is tacit rather than explicit. Approaches are taken for granted, skills assumed and things generally left unsaid. In the past this did not matter too much because students came from particular social back-grounds where such tacit knowledge was assumed. Professional families were familiar with the ethos of universities, and apprentices often knew someone who had trodden that particular path before them. With the expansion and diversification of education we can no longer rely on such tacit knowledge and therefore the need to spell out what is involved becomes greater.

Even if induction is provided, it may not work well. Formal meetings may be stiff and artificial. Introductions can be awkward. There may simply be too much information to take in. The real questions may not be addressed. Even if there is discussion, one or two voluble students may dominate. In the absence of effective induction, students may turn to one another or to the student grapevine, but that might not be reliable or up to date.

The need for induction is greatest where there is a step-change in the system: from GCSE to AS/A level, from school to further or higher educ-ation, academic to vocational study, taught course to research. Apparent continuities also carry risks in the sense that too much may be assumed about the links between one module or level and another. Two courses or modules may have similar titles but involve quite different levels or types of work in practice. However, the greatest obstacle to successful induction is simply our own familiarity with everything. We become so used to the course and the place that we forget what it is like to be a newcomer.

WHAT'S THE PROBLEM?

Depending on the nature of the problem and the situation you are in, consider the following:

- Do not forget the need for basic, physical orientation: where rooms and buildings are, how to get from A to B, toilets, car parking, crèches and so on. Provide for special needs. Do not underestimate how lost people can feel the first time they are on a spread-out campus or in a large building. Provide simple maps, guides, and directions.
- Spell out the essential arrangements at the first meeting, for example: times, deadlines, venues. Check that everyone is clear about these.
- If you think it is appropriate, use name tags/table cards for the first few sessions until people get to know one another. Decide whether first or family names are to be used.
- Get people working in small groups (pairs, trios, quartets) at the beginning. This way they can establish initial relationships with a few other people, which can then widen out to include the rest of the group.
- Divide the group into pairs and ask each person to introduce the other, including one thing about them that has nothing to do with the course (eg, hobby or experience). That helps make them more three-dimensional as people and goes beyond the student role.
- Take time to deal with general questions in the first session or two and do not worry if you cannot cover as much ground as you planned; a good foundation will allow you to progress more quickly later.

- People cannot take it all in at the beginning, so set aside some time when the course has got going to check their understanding of the arrangements, ground rules and so on.
- Use previous or more experienced students to show new ones round, explain the course, or mentor them over a longer period.
- Check your pre-course or induction materials to make sure they are clear, not too wordy, and address the questions they should.
- Leave time either at the end of classes or at other times for individual students to ask you questions, which may reflect their own particular situation/problems/expectations and may require some privacy.
- Foreign students may need additional or different induction to help them get to grips with the nature of the course, the institution and the culture. Educational systems and styles of teaching, learning and assessment vary a good deal from one country to another. There may also be underlying differences in terms of the perceived authority of the teacher, attitudes to knowledge, conventions about working in groups, communication in the class and so on.
- Make sure that all health and safety issues are fully and rigorously addressed; failure to do so can have serious consequences for the students, you and the institution.

Note down below any solutions you have come up with, in the light of the COSTAS checklist (see pages 69–70).

A

SOLUTIONS

14 HAVE THEY GOT THE RESOURCES FOR LEARNING?

NO ☐   **?** ☐   **YES** ☐

One of the difficulties that faces people trying to learn something on their own is acquiring the necessary resources and materials. This is not simply a matter of getting hold of them, which can be difficult or expensive enough, but of identifying the right kinds of resources: right for the learner and for that particular learning task. Thus, one of the basic functions of any course is to provide students with an adequate range of materials, textbooks that are well written and pitched at the right level, good handouts, software that is accessible and appropriate, equipment that is modern and works properly and facilities that enable them to get on with learning without continually running into practical obstacles or difficulties. However, even if these resources are available there is the further question of whether the students have the necessary skills to make proper use of them.

- Have there been any complaints by students about learning materials, equipment or facilities?
- Have there been complaints by staff?
- Are there peaks in demand for certain kinds of resources?
- Do all students (eg, full-timers/part-timers/those on different sites/ at a distance) have equal access to learning resources?
- How adequate/accessible are the library resources for your course?
- How about the computing facilities?
- How reliable and up-to-date is the equipment you use?
- What about the general social facilities?

Most courses are more resource-based than they were even five years ago; they rely more heavily on prepared teaching and learning materials and the systems to support and deliver them. Whole courses are now provided through e-learning. In one way, this has been a great leap forward, and we have only to consider the range of off-the-shelf products now available and the amazing accessibility of material on the Web to realize just how rapidly such provision has grown. This is partly a consequence of the information and communications revolution. The development of resource-based learning may also reflect a shift away from teacher-led to student-managed learning, which may itself stem from deteriorating staff–student ratios, for example in higher education. Student-managed learning may well be desirable in itself for educational reasons, but it does throw a greater responsibility on the students to make good use of such resources, and that in turn implies certain strategies and skills (see Section 17). It also requires staff to be more explicit about the objectives and processes of teaching and learning than they may be in the face-to-face situation where they can rely on students picking up some of these things as they go along.

Resources are thus one of the success stories of contemporary education and their range, variety and often quality are astonishing. However, teachers may encounter three kinds of problems. The first is cost. Budgetary constraints have their most obvious effect on courses and subjects that depend heavily on equipment or special facilities. These include not only medicine, agriculture, science and engineering but also non-technical subjects such as catering, hairdressing, music, and art and design. Over time, a shortage of funds inevitably erodes the quality of resources in all fields, sometimes imperceptibly at first as teachers stagger on with ageing textbooks or students quietly pick up the bill and buy their own, but eventually in a manifest deterioration of quality.

The second problem is the opposite to the first: there is money but it is not well spent. Learning resources now play an increasing part in most courses, and one consequence has been the rise of a major industry geared to supplying such needs. This requires greater knowledge and discrimination than before on the part of purchasers if they are not to waste money on well-hyped but poor-quality or inappropriate products, both hardware and 'courseware'. Where in the past ordering could largely be left to individual staff, there is now a need to coordinate purchasing policy in order to ensure that systems and products are compatible and that the institution gets the best deal.

The third problem is peaks in demand. Rather like transport systems at rush hour, courses struggle to cope when everyone wants to get the same books from the library, or use the computer terminals or find some lab or workshop space at the same time. And however much one exhorts students to think and plan ahead, some always seem to leave things till the last minute.

WHAT'S THE PROBLEM?

Even though they may affect the teaching of courses, many resource issues have to be tackled at departmental or institutional rather than course level, so your responses to this section will depend very much on your own position in the institution. That said, here are some suggestions.

- Build in regular questions about resources and materials to student feedback questionnaires. It is important to get systematic information about their use, rather than rely on spontaneous, individual comments.
- Individual members of staff can develop specialist expertise in certain types or aspects of resources and then advise others on purchase and use (including for example issues of copyright or compatibility). This may involve periodic attendance at workshops and product fairs.
- Take advantage of any group purchasing schemes that are available. These may be organized regionally or by type of institution.
- One member of staff can take special responsibility for the needs of part-time students or others who may not get equal access to resources, and act as a point of contact for requests/complaints.

- Explore ways of smoothing out peaks in demand by (i) changing timetables, (ii) re-arranging the order of topics, or (iii) altering assignment deadlines.
- Place restrictions on the length of time students can use key books (short-loan) or occupy computer terminals.
- Give clear advice to students on what they need to buy for their own use and ensure that they know approximately how much this will cost in advance of enrolling on the course.
- Organize workshops for students on how to engage in resource-based learning; do not assume that they will have the necessary skills already. Provide follow-up support on any problems that arise.
- If one does not already exist, develop an agreed policy on student use of Internet sources in their assignments or other work in terms of acceptability, downloading, referencing and plagiarism.

Note down any solutions below with reference to the COSTAS checklist.

SOLUTIONS

15 IS THE COURSE MANAGEABLE?

NO ☐   ? ☐   YES ☐

A course should be manageable. It should make reasonable demands on students in terms of scope, level, integration, workload and timescale. The main responsibility for these elements lies with those who design and deliver the course, but the management of learning is always a shared matter, and particularly so in the post-school field. Even in schools, pupils or students need to plan and prioritize their work, manage their time, and organize themselves to deliver what is required of them. In higher education, students have to take even more responsibility for their own learning, and if they are working at a distance from the institution they have to be largely self-directing and self-managing. Students may find a course difficult but that is *not* the same as finding it unmanageable. The former is usually expressed in terms of learning or understanding; the latter is typically couched in terms of coping or surviving.

- Does the course cover too much/too little/the right amount?
- Do the various parts of the course hang together properly?
- Is the sequence of topics appropriate?
- Are there any problems of timing?
- How about the overall workload?
- Do students get the information they need to manage their learning?
- Do staff and students agree on the balance of responsibility for managing the course?
- Where several staff are involved in teaching the course, do they liaise properly and produce a coherent whole?

Management problems for students may stem from the design, organization or delivery of a course. The first is fundamental. If a course is badly designed – for example in terms of its scope, structure or sequence – it may be very difficult for teachers and students to cope with it. The most common problem with design is overload, which arises from the tendency of course planners to keep adding new topics without subtracting others.

As subjects and fields develop, there is a natural tendency to want to include the latest developments, which may sometimes reflect a current policy emphasis or flavour of the month. However, planners and teachers can also be loath to get rid of content and tend to hang on to what they know and perhaps studied themselves. Professional bodies can be guilty of this as well, and the consequence is a steadily increasing overload that then necessitates a radical review or overhaul every decade or so. Where courses are nationally or centrally designed, there may be little that lecturers or teachers can do about all this beyond shifting the order of topics or varying the relative emphasis on each.

Even a well-designed course may be poorly organized. This can give rise to any number of practical problems: sudden changes in plan, cancellations at short notice, problems with rooms or materials, rapid turnover of staff, lack of continuity, confusion about what is happening when. Where several staff are involved in teaching the course, there may be a lack of coordination or liaison that means that the different parts of the course are not well integrated. Poor organization may also show up in the quality of information that the students receive, which may be incomplete, inaccurate, conflicting or just late. And while it is important to consider the overall design and teaching of a course, do not neglect the everyday house-keeping, such as room or timetable changes, staff substitutions, deadlines, individual messages, return of assignments or notification of results. Small problems can add up to great frustrations.

Poor or selfish teaching can also make a course unmanageable. Teachers who impose idiosyncratic or unpredictable demands on students, who ignore what their colleagues are doing, or who take no account of norms or procedures can create problems that spread well beyond their own teaching and may have knock-on effects on an entire programme. These problems become most acute when they are related to assessment: unreasonable demands in one area can lead to students devoting too little attention to others and possibly underperforming in these. It is only the students who experience the course *as a whole*.

Students too have to play their part in managing a course. Problems can arise if they are not used to doing this, and sometimes the transition from one level or sector to another involves a change in their role and responsibilities that they may not be aware of or ready for. Managing one's own learning involves certain skills to do with planning, organizing, time management (especially in terms of assignments), networking and getting feedback, and again students may not be conscious of the need to develop these.

WHAT'S THE PROBLEM?

Here are some ideas:

- Build questions about the design of the course into the student feedback forms or process.
- Discuss and agree the ground rules for managing the course with the students, especially if they are new to this type or level of work. Review how the course is going with them about half way through.
- Run workshops for students on managing their learning or point them to study support services if they are available.
- If you have any control over it, reconsider the design of the course about every third cycle. If there seems to be a problem of overload, divide the course content into 'must cover', 'should cover' and 'could cover'.

- Organize the course around aims and objectives rather than content or topics. This will usually lead to a leaner and fitter curriculum than a content-driven one.
- Where several people are involved in teaching the course, assign someone to coordinate it (unless you all work really well as a team).
- Ask personal tutors or supervisors what problems students are having. Ask secretaries or support staff also. Students often go to them for information, so they will often have their ear to the ground in a way you may not.
- Check the course handbook or other materials to ensure that they answer the kinds of questions the students actually ask.

See also Section 17 on student learning and Sections 23 and 24 on assessment. The whole of Chapter 3 is about the management of teaching and many of the points there lie behind the issues raised in this section. Now try to identify some solutions. The most relevant COSTAS headings are likely to be cost, organization, staff and students.

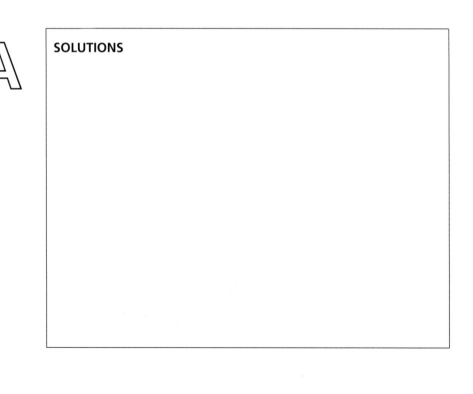

SOLUTIONS

16   IS THE COURSE WELL DELIVERED?

NO ☐   **?** ☐   **YES** ☐

Even if a course assembles the necessary learning resources in a manageable way, it still has to be delivered. Delivery involves bringing the students into contact and engagement with what they have to learn. A well-delivered course will use the most appropriate 'package' or mix of methods, media and materials to do this, and use them skilfully. The word 'appropriate' implies that there is no general pattern here, and the forms of delivery will depend on the kind of course you and your colleagues are teaching, in terms of its general aims, the nature of the content, the level of work, the numbers and types of students, the physical setting, the institutional context and the prevailing educational norms in the system or culture (see Notes). Delivery becomes a problem where the means used are inappropriate in respect of one or more of the above. And even if the means or methods used are appropriate, they have to be applied competently and well.

- What are the main means used for delivering the course?
- Have these changed recently? Are further changes contemplated?
- Are the staff comfortable with the methods they are using?
- Do the students prefer some kinds of activities to others?
- Do the students prefer some teachers to others?
- Have any delivery problems emerged from student feedback?
- Ideally, if there were no constraints of time, money or staffing, how would you deliver the course?

Typically, a course will involve some form of communication to *large groups*, through lecturing, presentations, demonstrations or other forms of whole-class teaching. This is usually one-way, though it may be interspersed with questions, quizzes or other activities. A course will also usually involve some *small group* work such as paired or shared tasks, buzz-groups, role play, seminars or discussions. It may have an *individualized* element as well in the shape of one-to-one tutorials, supervision or coaching, though some of this may be informal and take place outside the class.

Depending on the nature of the subject, there may be *practical* components such as workshops, skill sessions, laboratory periods, rehearsals, simulations, visits, field trips, work-shadowing or on-the-job placements. The picture is usually completed by an element of *private study* in terms of follow-up work, reading, homework exercises, essays, reports, projects or other assignments. Problems can arise with any of the above, and it may be useful to run down the list in your mind, asking yourself which go well and which seem to work less well and for what reason. Do problems occur because you or other staff are inexperienced in or unhappy with using that particular method or approach? Do numbers make it difficult? Do the students not respond well to that activity? Courses always involve a mixture of methods, and it may be that the balance is not quite right, that you need more of one thing and less of something else. But is that realistic in the circumstances?

Technology now allows us to employ many of these methods indirectly or at a distance, or to substitute resource-based learning for face-to-face contact. Some 'courseware' can be bought off the shelf, while other forms may need to be developed in-house. Either way, there is usually an initial investment hump of money or time, but the pay-off over time can be considerable. So you may need to consider the potential role of technology in delivery and the way in which it might be used to solve some current problems. Equally, you may need to address problems that the technology itself creates, such as isolating students as they work in their own time and at their own pace, undermining the collective support of the group and weakening the everyday contact between them and staff.

However, the main barrier to addressing delivery problems is likely to be *you yourself*. We all identify with what we do and may invest a good deal of pride and self-respect in our teaching, especially if we have been doing it reasonably well for some time. So it is not always easy for us (or our colleagues) to take on board criticisms or suggestions about how we might do things differently. Teaching is a complex activity, not only cognitively but emotionally; we need to be immersed in it to do it well, but also to stand back from it in order to analyse it. This means that you have to think carefully about how you and your colleagues are supported in making any changes in your methods that may be needed, and how you can develop an ethos that is at once critical but constructive. After all, that is how we are meant to help students too.

Which leads on to the final point. Teaching is not just a matter of methods and techniques. It has to do with *being there for the student*. This more personal aspect is more difficult to pin down but is none the less real for that. In your analysis of the delivery of the course, it is therefore important to explore what you and the other teachers mean for the students, what significance you have and how they would miss you if you went. If they would.

WHAT'S THE PROBLEM?

Here are some ideas:

- Analyse student feedback about delivery, not just for the last course but previous ones as well, so that you get a more represent-ative view. You may get a 'blip' with one particular group.
- Include some more general questions about the role and signif-icance of the teachers for the students, in terms of stimulus, example, support. How much do you mean to them? (See also Section 18 on modelling and Section 19 on support.)
- If you do not obtain student feedback regularly, conduct a one-off survey about their responses to different methods and activities. By implication, this may identify different teachers, so it may need sensitive handling.
- Sit in on one another's sessions, both to give feedback to your colleagues and to learn from what they do. It is important that this is seen as a two-way process, so have two columns on your page: What can I tell you from watching you? And what did I learn from watching you?

● Set aside regular occasions (if time and money allow, an 'awayday') just to explore the delivery of the course. Invite the participants to nominate topics for discussion. Focus on what works as well as what does not. Find out what is done in other places. Bring in an outsider to stop it getting too cosy or inbred.
● Assign one member of staff to keep up-to-speed with new software products in the field (learning packages, Web links) so that he or she can inform everyone else. This is quite time-consuming, and may also involve some travel and therefore cost.
● Designate one or more members of staff who are interested anyway in computers to develop special expertise in the educational uses of technology, and ask them to help and advise everyone else.
● If individual members of staff seem to have special experience or talents in particular forms of delivery (eg, presentation, role play) invite them to demonstrate or pass these on to their colleagues. There will always be a mix of strengths in any teaching team; use them.
● Check the link between delivery and assessment to make sure that the way you assess students is not contradicting, skewing or undermining the way you try to teach them.

Make a note below of any solutions. Do not forget COSTAS.

SOLUTIONS

17 DO THE STUDENTS KNOW HOW TO GO ABOUT THEIR STUDIES?

NO ☐   ? ☐   YES ☐

Teaching–learning is always a partnership. The teacher's expertise in teaching has to be complemented by the student's expertise in learning. While much thought and effort have gone into training teachers how to teach, much less goes into the latter: indeed, learning to learn is usually seen as a natural spin-off of learning X, Y or Z. It is widely assumed that by the time students come to the end of compulsory education, they will have picked up or found out how to learn. Otherwise how would they have got that far? There is some truth in this but the relatively high rates of non-completion or failure in some areas of post-school education (particularly FE) suggest that we need to take learning to learn more seriously. That need is also evident in the years leading up to GCSE in secondary school, as students prepare for major, public tests of their achievement. And uncertainty about, or lack of self-confidence in, learning may also deter some adults from embarking on courses that they might otherwise attend. Thus where the previous section explored the teacher's problems of delivery, this one looks at the other side of the coin: the student's capacity to learn.

- Do the students know how to approach the course?
- Do they understand the kinds of tasks they are set?
- What do they think 'learning' is?
- Do they read or misread the learning situation?
- Do they have the essential study skills?
- Can they get on with work on their own?
- Do they work productively in groups?
- What about their exam or assessment technique?
- Can they manage their own learning?

Like teaching, learning has three basic dimensions. The most fundamental of these is the learner's view of learning – what he or she thinks learning is. After all, learning is a broad term and one may understand it in various ways, for example as memorizing, as absorbing, as following, as applying, as interpreting, as creating. . . The same applies to the learning environment. Some students may think they should simply do what the teacher says, while others may expect to use their own initiative; some may expect to focus on the subject matter, while others may expect to develop their own ideas. Prior experience may teach students to take a greater or lesser degree of responsibility for their own learning, and you may inherit these assumptions. 'Learning' is itself an open concept, and it is important that the students understand it in the appropriate way, whatever that is, since this will determine their general approach.

Second, learning involves 'reading' the task and interpreting the situation. In the early part of a course, students may spend a good deal of time and effort on working out what is expected or needed, what the ground rules are, what particular teachers are like, how much work they really have to do, how strict the deadlines are, how the assessment system actually operates and so on. They also need to work out what each assignment is really about and how to approach it, what mistakes to avoid, what to emphasize or highlight, and how to present it. Failure to do these things can lead to misdirected or wasted effort, and beyond that to a more serious, fundamental misreading of the whole learning situation.

Third, learning, like teaching, involves practical skills. The methods and skills of the teacher assume complementary methods and skills on the part of the learner. If I give a lecture, the students need to be able to take notes. If they have a lot to read, they need to develop reading strategies. If there is a discussion, they need to be able to communicate with me and one another. If I set an assignment, they need to be able to find the material, structure their ideas and write it. If they have a project to do, they need to be able to search databases, locate sources, structure their outline, plan ahead and so on. Beyond such specific skills, they also need to be able to manage their time and the other general aspects of the course (see Section 15). There are also skills and techniques related to specific forms of assessment: how to tackle multiple-choice tests, how to choose which question to answer, how to organize a long essay, how to check calculations, how to cope with an oral exam and so on.

Many books on learning to learn concentrate on such skills and techniques, perhaps because they are concrete and specific, but the ability to interpret the learning task and read the learning situation are just as important (see Note for page 63). Underlying the whole process is the student's conception of learning that will lead him or her, consciously or not, to adopt a particular approach. Problems with learning can relate to any of these three dimensions, though the third (skills) is more obvious than the second (interpretation), which in turn is easier to diagnose than the first (conception). Finally, do not forget that students' approaches to learning are heavily influenced not only by how they are taught but by the way they are assessed.

WHAT'S THE PROBLEM?

Here are some solutions to think about.

- Discuss the whole topic of 'learning to learn' with your colleagues. It is important to discover what everyone's views are, since there may be personal, implicit differences of emphasis that in turn influence the students' work in practice. You need to agree on some common approaches.
- Set out the expected learning approaches and skills in the course handbook or other material, but do not rely on everyone reading this or taking it in.
- Discuss the nature of the course and its ground rules with the students early on. It is particularly important to do this if the course marks a new stage or transition for them. Return to the key issues about half way through the course in order to reinforce the message and resolve any questions that may have arisen by that stage.

- Spend some time explaining the ground rules for the first assignment or substantial piece of work and feeding back on it afterwards. This should pay off in terms of fewer errors or inappropriate strategies in subsequent work.
- If there seem to be some common learning skills that are lacking, for example to do with reading, locating material, note-taking or planning work, organize a workshop or surgery to deal with them. Perhaps allow students to opt into those bits they think they need, but give some general advice as well, especially to those whom you think may need it.
- Find some published material that will give students guidance on common study strategies and skills – there is lots available – or if you have a central study advice service, use it.
- Give students some 'model' exercises or assignments and explain to them why they are good.
- Give them a range of such work and ask them to assess it. Discuss the criteria that emerge. This should help them to become aware of the kind of approach that is needed.
- Form students into subgroups and ask them to identify the learning problems they have. This allows individuals to shelter behind the group response and should encourage them to be more open.
- Encourage students to keep a learning diary or log and then discuss what emerges from this after a month or two, allowing individuals to disclose to the group only what they choose to. This is a major exercise in terms of time and commitment, but can be worthwhile as a long-term investment in self-awareness and autonomous learning.
- If you think your students could cope with this, work through the 11 functions of teaching set out in Chapter 1 with them. Explain each one and discuss the extent to which they are your or their responsibility (see Appendix 2). This is quite a demanding exercise but will equip them to understand their own learning in a way that should benefit them in the longer term. After all, if we are serious about 'learning to learn' we need to invest some time and effort in it, and so do the learners.

In terms of the COSTAS checklist many of the above solutions will cost little and have minimal impact on the organization. The most relevant headings are likely to be staff and students and in some cases time.

A

SOLUTIONS

18 ARE THE TEACHERS GOOD MODELS?

NO ☐   ? ☐   YES ☐

Students learn not just from what teachers say and do but what they are. Modelling, in this sense, can be an important though sometimes unconscious or unacknowledged part of teaching. Its importance varies with the type of course. In school, the teacher may represent the grown up, the adult. In vocational or professional education, he or she may exemplify the experienced or skilled practitioner-role; after all one *is* a doctor or designer or mechanic. In higher education, the lecturer may embody the subject and make it come alive. In the creative or performing arts, models may constitute an essential stage on the long journey to finding one's own style or voice. Modelling is not central to all courses, and even where it is, the model may be ignored or rejected (I hope I never become like him. . .). However, it is more subtle and pervasive than we sometimes admit (think of the teachers or lecturers who influenced you in the past), so we need to address it as an aspect of teaching that can have quite profound and lasting effects on the learner, both positive and negative. After all, as the advertisement said: 'nobody forgets a good teacher' (rather than teaching).

- How important is modelling in your general role as a teacher (not at all/a bit/a good deal/very)?
- How important is modelling as a process in learning your subject?
- Do you feel comfortable with the idea of being a model for your students?
- Do the students look for models of what they are studying?
- Are they exposed to negative models on the course?
- Are there conflicting models?
- Do they go elsewhere for their models?
- Are they models for one another?
- Do they no longer need models?

Modelling involves paying attention to, imitating and internalizing some aspect of the behaviour of a significant other person. It may be a deliberate or unconscious process. It can also be positive or negative. Models are usually people we know, but they can also be personalities we know of at a distance, for example through the media. They might be charismatic public figures or individuals who are a familiar part of our family or work environment. Leadership often involves some element of modelling.

Education is fertile ground for modelling simply because of the conditions that exist there. Teachers are usually older than students. They have power and authority over them and can deploy rewards or sanctions. They interact with their students repeatedly, sometimes daily, over a period of time, sometimes years. That interaction is intense, concentrated. They talk while students listen, do things while the students watch. They operate in closed environments. The very idea of teaching implies that students have something to learn from them. The institution invests teachers with a certain status that is often (though not always) reinforced by the wider society. It is no wonder that teachers often loom large in the memory – as the Friends Reunited Web site testifies!

Modelling can become a problem for three reasons. First, the fact that it is often unconscious, operating somewhere below the level of rational control, raises questions about student identity and autonomy. Do teachers have the right to act as models? Should students be influenced in this way? How do we square this with the idea that education is about thinking for yourself and becoming your own person? Second, there may be conflicting models. For example, lecturers may represent one kind of approach and practitioners another. How is the student to reconcile these differing examples? Third, the model may be inappropriate or negative; it may embody values, attitudes or processes that for one reason or another we think undesirable (but who is to say?).

The first thing is to decide how important modelling is in your situation or on your kind of course. If after reading this you still think it is marginal or inappropriate then you should move on to the next section, although it may be worth asking your students; after all, they are on the receiving end, and you might get a surprise. If you believe it is an issue, you need to consider which of the three kinds of problems described above may exist. Or you may think that it should be explored further for some other reason. Modelling is one of the more subtle and sensitive aspects of teaching and learning, and it is not always easy to 'surface' it. But ignoring or denying it will not make it go away.

WHAT'S THE PROBLEM?

Here are some ideas:

- Analyse your own experience. Did certain teachers or lecturers have a particular influence on you? If so, in what ways? Think of two or three examples.
- Case studies or autobiographical accounts by other teachers or students offer another useful way into the subject, and one that provides a degree of detachment from the immediate, personal case.
- Conflicting models (for example between theorists and practitioners) can be discussed in terms of the different contexts of their work rather than just different people. We are as we are partly because of the worlds we live in, and the world of (say) the teacher/academic may be rather different from that of the practitioner in a field such as nursing, business or engineering.
- Students themselves can offer very perceptive accounts of the process since they have direct experience of it. It may be useful to introduce some of the basic concepts of modelling to give them a framework for discussion, so that it does not simply degenerate into personalities and cases (see Notes).
- Simulations and role plays can be used to act out aspects of modelling, but it is important both to provide a clear initial briefing about the purpose of the exercise and to debrief it carefully again at the end. The activity in itself is not enough.

- Modelling can form part of the informal 'hidden curriculum' of teaching (see Note for page 21), so it is important to analyse formal course documents to see how the process of modelling relates to aims and outcomes. Is there any explicit reference to modelling in course materials? If not, why not? Is it perhaps too personal or sensitive an issue?
- Try to identify the affective (related to values, attitudes or feelings) objectives of your course. They may be embedded in processes and practices, and difficult to articulate (see Notes).
- As always, have a look at the assessment criteria and methods to see if they raise any questions about this aspect of the course. Are certain models implicitly reinforced or penalized? How does all this affect marking or grading, if it does?

Of the COSTAS checklist, modelling is most likely to raise issues for staff *and* students.

SOLUTIONS

The next section on *support* also has a strong affective element.

19 DO THE STUDENTS GET THE SUPPORT THEY NEED?

NO ☐   ? ☐   YES ☐

Not all learning problems have to do with learning. It is one thing not to follow some part of a lecture or understand an equation or know how to perform a particular skill. These are the kinds of problems inherent in learning, and indeed learning can be seen as the process of overcoming them. However, it is another thing to lose confidence, feel you are going round in circles, or to become alienated from the whole business of education. Learning is not just a matter of specifics; it also involves general factors such as motivation, energy level, self-esteem and a sense of identity, purpose and direction. Some of these may reflect changes outside the learning situation altogether: money worries, the breakdown of a relationship, drugs, problems at work, illness or the general shifts of priority and circumstance that may occur during adolescent or adult life. Students thus need guidance and support in both the narrower sense of help with particular difficulties and the broader sense of sustaining their general will to learn. Students with additional difficulties or problems, whether physical, psychological, linguistic or social, will need additional support.

- What kinds of learning problems do students typically encounter on the course?
- What other kinds of problem do they run into?
- How do you become aware of either kind of problem?
- Are there distinct subgroups of students and associated problems, for example in terms of age, background, gender, family or work situation, or mode of study?
- Is there a pattern of truancy/dropout/failure? What are the reasons?
- To whom do the students generally turn for support?
- Is there a designated tutorial/personal supervision system, and if so does it work?
- What special forms of support does the institution provide for those who need them?

The key question does not specifically mention teachers. That is because students may turn to various people – family, friends, classmates, colleagues – as well as teaching staff for the guidance and support they want. Indeed, if the latter are part of the problem the students will certainly look elsewhere. The question also refers to the support students *need*. This is because the situation will vary from one student to another and because in some cases students will be (and may be expected to be) largely self-reliant and capable of sorting things out for themselves. A lot depends on the ethos of the institution; some students prefer further education to school precisely because it is more anonymous, and university students often want to get away from home. Variations in attitudes will also be found among staff, and students usually sense quite quickly who will listen and who will not. Sometimes an unofficial source of support will be more helpful than the officially designated tutor.

Support is quite a tricky issue. On the one hand, there is a widespread expectation in this country that those who work in education will not just help with the kinds of cognitive problems mentioned at the beginning but address the wider emotional and personal difficulties that may affect students' learning and welfare. However, that expectation has to be set against the need to refer students on for professional help when it is necessary. Not all teachers are capable of, or comfortable with, providing such support. The control and authority that teachers have bring with them certain obligations to look after those in their charge, but the tradition of pastoral care is stronger in some post-compulsory sectors than others (try placing schools, sixth form colleges, further education, higher education, adult education and training on a 'spectrum of care'). It is also stronger in some countries than others. And while educational institutions in the UK usually provide direct or indirect access to professional counselling services students may prefer to talk to someone they already know through their everyday studies rather than make a formal appointment to see a stranger, however professional.

What is important in the end is that they get the necessary support from somewhere, and this may come from their peers or families as well as from teachers or other professionals. It is when students do not get adequate support from any source that problems arise, and unfortunately this may not become evident until too late, that is, when the person has already dropped out, or become completely disillusioned or worse. The need for support thus requires some individual and institutional sensitivity in both identifying and dealing with problems, and a kind of early warning system.

The growth of choices within courses and programmes that is one consequence of modularization also creates an increased need for educational guidance at interim stages (Which modules should I opt for? What future options do they underpin or preclude?) and many students will need access to careers guidance during or at the end of their studies.

WHAT'S THE PROBLEM?

Here are some ideas:

- Leave 'windows' open for students to talk to you, for example during a break, at the end of a class, or meeting in the corridor. Do not just hurry on.
- If you can, set aside regular 'surgery' hours when students can come and talk to you, but also be ready to see them at short notice in an emergency.
- Be aware that students may 'present' with an apparently minor problem but in fact want to talk about a more serious one. Allow them the opportunity during the conversation to move on to this (Is there anything else. . .?).
- Set a short piece of work early on. This will not only help you to identify specific content difficulties, but also give you a natural pretext for talking to students individually if you think that there may be other problems.

- Establish an early warning system for picking up emerging difficulties. Have a staff meeting soon after the start of the course simply to pool information and identify any students who seem to be running into problems.
- Group tutorials in the early stages can be as good as or better than individual ones, and also less time consuming. They enable students to see that they are not alone in having problems, allow them to develop mutual support, and are less daunting than a one-to-one encounter with a lecturer or teacher may be.
- Make sure that all staff are familiar with the relevant procedures, know what specialist help is available and how they can refer students to support services. Make students aware of such services too, perhaps as part of their initial induction.
- Carry out a simple survey of the personal tutorial system if there is one. Ask students whether it works.
- Communication between staff is crucial. It is essential that messages about possible problems are passed on and you may need to formalize some kind of process to ensure that such things do not fall through the net.

While most of the above ideas concern staff and students, there may also be organizational implications in some cases.

SOLUTIONS

20   DO THE STUDENTS LEARN FROM ONE ANOTHER?

NO ☐   ? ☐   YES ☐

Most education takes place in groups: classes, forms, sets or intakes. This makes it more difficult to give individuals the attention they need and deserve, especially when the groups are large, and so we are sometimes reduced to 'teaching towards the middle' or other compromises. However, it also has a plus side in that the group may itself become a vehicle for learning. At the most basic level, it establishes a regular rhythm and pattern of work that might be difficult for individuals to maintain on their own. Students can learn from one another and support one another (see Section 19) in pairs, trios or other small clusters in or outside the class. They may form a bond, sometimes against the teacher, usually against the examiners. They will revise together. Rote learning can be carried out by hearing and testing one another's vocabulary, lists or formulae. Peer learning can also take more interesting forms, in which students share exercises, discuss topics and problems, or work together on a project. The potential for this kind of learning depends on the subject matter, and some teachers and educational cultures favour it more than others. However, modern educational practice tends to encourage teachers to explore the potential of peer or cooperative learning, partly as a strategy for coping with large numbers, partly as a means of sharing meanings, and partly as a reflection of the way people work in the wider world.

- Do the students work together spontaneously?
- Are they deliberately encouraged to work together?
- Does the subject matter permit peer learning?
- Are the learning tasks typically ones they can share?
- Is the group competitive or collaborative?
- Do some students seem rather isolated? If so, why?
- Does the pattern of assessment promote or inhibit peer learning?
- Are teamwork and cooperation important aims of the course?

Peer learning is affected by a wide range of factors: the nature and difficulty of the subject matter, the relationships between students, their individual preferences, the general ethos of the group, the attitude of the teacher, the norms of the educational and wider culture, the pattern of assessment, and ultimately the purpose of the course. So it may or may not be an important aspect of your teaching, and the first question is to decide whether it should be. You might have particular reasons for wanting individuals to work on their own (to ensure that each person actually covers everything) or for controlling the flow of information (to ensure that it is accurate and that the procedures are correct) or for having individual assessment (to control plagiarism or monitor minimum standards). Behind such concerns sometimes lie imperatives of competency, safety or professional requirements, and behind those again the possibility of litigation.

However, you may want to encourage peer learning but still find it difficult to do so. A good deal will depend on the abilities, attitudes and expectations students bring to the course, and whether they are used to working in this way. Pressure of time may also force you to take the initiative through didactic or directive teaching in order to cover the ground; you cannot monitor what they are talking about in all those little groups, and they may be wasting valuable time. Moreover, the students themselves can become impatient and want to hear it from you. After all, you are the teacher, aren't you? You have the expertise. And they may be paying for it.

Assessment is also a powerful influence on the way people work, and despite the fact that much teaching is collective, most assessment is individual. That contradiction is not lost on students who reason that at the end of the day it is they who are on the line, not their group. On the other hand, teachers can forget what it is like not to understand, and sometimes one's peers are better at explaining things. One variation on peer learning has more experienced students (say from the next year or stage) tutoring the current ones. The advantage of this is that while such students have now mastered the topic, they still remember what it was like to learn it.

The recent growth of resource-based learning using software and print-based packages also raises interesting questions about peer learning. Do such materials tend to isolate students, as they work at their own pace at their own level in their own place? Or is the technology used to enhance interaction and exchange, through networks, chat-rooms and the like? The technology is now flexible enough to serve whatever purpose we want; the question is how we want to use it.

WHAT'S THE PROBLEM?

Here are some ideas to consider:

- Back off a little. Stop 'teaching' all the time and let the group or groups get on with it. Have faith, trust them a bit. But give them some ground rules at the start to help them work together.
- Build up the interaction gradually. Have them working in pairs first, then put the pairs together in fours, and so on. That way, they will establish working relationships in smaller units before broadening out into the arena of the whole group.
- Encourage them to work together on subgroup tasks in the session. It may be better not to specify in advance who is to report back, so that everyone prepares and no one gets a free ride.
- Get groups to do presentations. Allow them to sort out who will be responsible for what.
- Encourage them to work together outside class. Do not let the fear of plagiarism banish all cooperation.
- Run a workshop for students on peer learning. This will take time but save time later. Introduce the basic ideas and discuss the pros and cons. Students, like teachers, need some preparation for new methods; you shouldn't just drop them in at the deep end.

- If teamwork is the natural or necessary mode of work in your field or occupation, reconstitute the whole class as 'learning sets' (of about five) who operate permanently together through all the stages of the work, from reading through activities to outputs.
- Reconsider the pattern of assessment to encourage peer work, for example in projects. It may be better to have both a group mark and individual marks to ensure that individual contributions are suitably rewarded.
- Consider some peer assessment as part of the overall assessment. This is a tricky area, so make sure that the ground rules are absolutely clear, and if necessary build in some quality assurance by staff. Make sure that it does not fall foul of any wider institutional or national assessment regulations.

Which headings in the COSTAS checklist do you think are most relevant to this topic?

SOLUTIONS

21 IS THERE A GOOD LEARNING ENVIRONMENT?

NO ☐   **?** ☐   **YES** ☐

Learning can take place almost anywhere, and there is now a good deal of evidence that much informal learning happens in the workplace, the home or virtually any other setting one can think of (see Notes). The point about education, however, is that it aims to create a dedicated learning environment, one that in the classroom, course or institution prioritizes learning above any other activity. The learning that takes place there may not be very different from that which occurs elsewhere, but it should be more intensive and effective. Such an environment should facilitate the learning process in every way and eliminate (as far as possible) the barriers or obstacles that typically face the informal learner. That said, dedicated educational environments may not in fact match these ideals, and may indeed create barriers of their own that are, paradoxically, the obverse of their very purpose. They may be dysfunctional in a variety of ways, all of which hinder rather than help the students in their learning.

- What is the physical environment like? Is it pleasant? Is it safe? Is it convenient?
- Does the institution provide a good social environment?
- Does the course offer a good learning environment?
- Do the students contribute to or undermine that environment?
- Is there anything that distracts staff from their teaching?
- Is there anything that gets in the way of effective learning?
- Ideally, would you change the learning environment in any way?

The learning environment has physical, organizational and educational aspects. The first is the most obvious, and one can quickly see the state of the buildings and rooms and the quality of the facilities. Although teachers and students can sometimes do good work in poor surroundings, there is no good reason why they should have to put up with conditions that are worse than they would have in the outside world. Apart from anything else, the state of the physical environment sends out messages about the relative priority accorded to education that must in the long run affect teachers' and students' attitudes to it. For example, both staff and students may feel that a college annexe is second best, although sometimes such buildings develop their own strong identity if they house a distinct unit or department.

The organizational environment has a more direct impact on teaching and learning in that it affects the running of the course and the day-to-day quality of the students' experience. Paradoxically, the student may notice the organization least when it is working best; it is when things go wrong (conflicting information, messages not passed on, confusion over arrangements, delays and general cock-ups) that the organization (or lack of it) becomes visible. Poor organization can affect everything from admissions through materials and teaching to assessment, and many of the background questions are raised in Chapter 3.

It is, however, the quality of the educational environment that matters most. At a minimum, a learning environment should not interfere with or impede learning or prevent students getting on with their work. That might sound absurd in institutions that are supposed to be dedicated to education, but it can happen because of classroom discipline or behaviour problems that mean teachers have to spend most of their time managing the class and cannot actually get round to much teaching. This is more of a problem at the compulsory stage, but can also occur in the immediate post-compulsory years (ie, 16–18) with students who are totally alienated from the whole idea of education; in particular, FE colleges are often asked to 'pick up the pieces' and provide for such groups.

A different problem arises when groups are so large and impersonal that it is virtually impossible for the teacher to take account of individual differences of aptitude or progress, either in the class or in marking work. It can also be the result of a rapid turnover of staff, which leads to a breakdown of continuity. It can happen because the teachers themselves are distracted from teaching by other things, such as paperwork or general administration, or because the institutional priorities actually have to do with activities other than teaching, such as research or consultancy.

By contrast a good learning environment is one in which students get that subtle blend of stimulus and security, challenge and support that helps bring about learning. This involves not only the teaching staff but also ancillary staff – receptionists, secretaries, technicians, librarians – indeed everyone who comes into contact with the student. It also requires a concern with the student not only during but before and after the course.

It implies treating the student as a person, not just a number or statistic. All this is basic in terms of 'customer care' in any commercial organization, but how much more so in one that is dealing with a fundamental human process such as education.

The way in which such an environment is created and sustained depends partly on the type of student and mode of study: full time, part time or at a distance, residential or non-residential. Overseas or visiting students will need special attention, as will those who have special needs. Split-site or multi-campus institutions have their own characteristics and problems. The nature of the environment also depends on the character of the institution. As noted earlier, some students deliberately opt out of school sixth forms because they want the more 'adult' atmosphere of a college; some students prefer to live in or live out of institutions. Different universities and colleges aim to provide different kinds of experience.

> **WHAT'S THE PROBLEM?**

Here are some ideas to think about (some of which will depend on your own position in the institution):

- Build some general questions about the learning environment into students' feedback forms. Allow the students to mention anything they want.
- If you can get funds to do it, carry out a survey of those who have finished the course some time afterwards (eg, three or six months)

and ask them about the quality of the learning environment. While they may have forgotten many of the specifics of the course, they will usually have formed a general impression of the whole experience by then.

- See if there are any small changes you can make in the physical environment that would not cost much but that would help to improve it. Even minor alterations can sometimes make a big difference.
- Have a suggestions box somewhere that students and staff can contribute to, anonymously if they wish. You may get some silly or offensive material, but also some useful items that can help to pinpoint more practical problems and solutions.
- Behaviour/discipline problems in the classroom have to be dealt with by a general policy and not left to individual teachers to try to cope with; otherwise disruptive students will exploit what they see as easy prey. If this is an issue, organize staff meetings to address it. Make problem students (and parents) realize they are taking on the whole institution.
- One member of staff can look after the interests of special groups of students who might otherwise get less attention or miss out, such as part-timers, mature students, those with young children, or linguistic minorities.
- Do not underestimate extra-curricular activities such as sport, societies and clubs. They may take up staff time but they help to create a more complete environment.
- It is important for students to have places where they can meet informally since this is partly how they create a community. It is equally important for staff; a lot of business can get done informally over lunch or coffee.
- If you do not have them already, consider organizing some social events, but involve the students in the thinking and planning.
- The most radical solution is to allow students to opt out of the educational environment altogether and get experience of the workplace or community: the 'real world'. That is likely to be a matter not just of institutional but national policy, but you may be able to build in shorter periods of work experience, placements or visits by developing links with local employers and communities.

Ideas such as the last clearly have organizational implications. But which of the COSTAS headings do the others involve?

SOLUTIONS

The next section goes beyond the institution altogether to ask about the wider community. You may not be able to do much about this aspect of your work, but it does impinge on courses and teaching in a number of ways, and relates back to previous sections on motivation (7) and self-belief (8) in particular.

22 IS EDUCATION VALUED IN THE WIDER COMMUNITY?

NO ☐   **?** ☐   **YES** ☐

Education does not take place in a vacuum. The wider culture permeates the classroom and the course through the kind of language used, the patterns of communication, the relationships between those involved, and the norms and expectations of both students and staff. However, the most important aspect of this community influence is the prevailing attitude to education and the value placed upon it. When education is valued, students are encouraged to enrol or attend, to work hard and achieve what they can. Staff likewise feel supported and respected. Where, by contrast, the community is apathetic about, dismissive of or even hostile to education, the job of both students and staff becomes much harder. In addition to the intrinsic difficulties of learning and teaching, staff have to cope with low esteem, lack of respect, persistent disruption and sometimes outright abuse and aggression.

- Are the students' parents interested in their education?
- Do local employers see the importance of education and training?
- Do different parts of the community value education differently?
- How is education treated in the local media?
- Do you feel that the government values education enough?
- Do you think education is valued more or less in other countries you know?
- As a teacher, do you feel that you are swimming with or against the tide?

The relationship between education and the community depends on both what we mean by education and what we mean by community. Few communities are homogeneous and we may need to distinguish between different socio-economic groups, different subcultures that may reflect ethnic, linguistic or religious diversities, different age groups, gender, and differences of domicile (inner city, urban, suburban, rural). In other words, community perceptions of and attitudes towards education are likely to vary considerably, although the location and catchment of a school or college may well mean that there is a dominant group or ethos. Since universities typically take in a much wider geographical spread of students, local factors will be relatively less important, but the student body may exhibit certain characteristics and patterns that affect teaching and assessment.

The education–community relationship also depends on the kind of education. Attitudes may vary not only in terms of the type of institution (school, college, university, adult education centre and so on) but in terms of subject. The latter may variously be regarded as difficult, easy, accessible, inaccessible, practical, academic, useful, irrelevant or fashionable. Some subjects may be highly respected; others, especially the more innovative ones, may be dismissed by some people as not proper subjects at all. Thus parents, employers and others may put pressure on students to opt for or concentrate on certain kinds of courses, and students themselves may have deeply embedded views about the importance or value of studying this or that. Individuals and communities may also vary in terms of the relative emphasis they place on qualifications. They may be less interested in what goes on during the course than in the end result, and the social status or job prospects that are attached to it.

In social terms, education is both a coercive and consenting activity. Legislation requires children to be educated, and for most of them that means school, where in turn they are subject to numerous rules and requirements. Even after the end of compulsory education, there may be strong pressures to participate. Employers and professional bodies may also stipulate certain training requirements. On the other hand, learning is a voluntary activity and teaching depends on the daily consent of those involved. If this is withheld, for whatever reason, teaching can seem a very uphill task.

WHAT'S THE PROBLEM?

Education–community relations are likely to be handled at the top of the institution and thus lie beyond your remit or power, but there are some things you can do at the level of the course or the class:

- If the opportunity arises naturally during the course, discuss attitudes to education with your students. Treat it as a collective rather than individual issue, which it probably is. Don't just accept low esteem as a social given; analyse the reasons why education is valued or not valued in your particular community. There may be historical reasons for this (low skill area, high youth unemployment). You may find that there is a certain logic even in what the dissenters say.
- Try to find ways in which you and other teachers can contribute to the community or get a higher profile other than through teaching. This will help people to see that you are not 'just' teachers.
- The problem with most meetings with parents is that they are based on students' work, which may be problematic, or their behaviour, which will be. Try to create other events that have nothing to do with students' work to which parents can be invited or in which they can become involved. Get to know them, and let them get to know you, as people. Come out of role occasionally.
- Where possible, open up the buildings and facilities for community use out of hours. As well as sometimes bringing in revenue, this can generate goodwill and make the place seem less inaccessible and more familiar.

- Many parents and employers do not have much idea of what actually goes on in the classroom. If possible, invite small numbers of outsiders to sit in to see what actually happens there. This could have interesting effects not only on them but on the students also, not to mention yourself and your colleagues.
- Past students can be a useful resource in explaining to current ones what may happen after they finish the course, in terms of jobs or further study. Invite them in to give a talk. This can help with initial recruitment too.
- If you work in the training field, you will be more concerned with the value placed on training by the organization/employer than the community. Try to manage any distance or tension that grows up between the work culture and the training culture by keeping in touch with the employer; though some tension and/or distance may actually be necessary if training is to do its job.
- Do not ignore the local media. Usually they will only approach you if they think there is a story; approach them if you have something you want to say.

Solutions to this problem depend very much on the context of the institution, and you may be able to come up with local or specific ones that are not mentioned above but that meet the needs of your particular situation.

Do not forget COSTAS.

A | **SOLUTIONS**

Having explored a range of general aspects of the course – teaching, learning, modelling, interaction, environment, context – we now move on to assessment, looking first at the criteria and then at methods and procedures.

You may want to pause here and fill in the profile on page 134 up to this point, reflecting again on the previous sections as you do so.

23 ARE THE ASSESSMENT CRITERIA SATISFACTORY?

NO ☐   **?** ☐   **YES** ☐

Assessment has run like a thread through this book. It has come up in many of the previous sections, and forms one element of the COSTAS checklist. Assessment may not be the be-all and end-all of education, which is arguably the learning and development of the student, but it is often the most pivotal aspect of teaching, usually the most formal, and always the most sensitive. It constitutes the formal currency or validation of learning, which is important both in terms of selection (for progression to further study or employment) and protection (as a licence to practise safely or competently). It refers back to the original aims or purpose of the course, and draws together all the aspects of its delivery such as methods, materials and environment. It can shape students' approach to learning, affect their motivation and provide feedback (though sometimes too late). It also offers a measure of the output or efficiency of a course, although as we shall see in Section 26 only a partial or incomplete one. As noted before, assessment is thus in one sense the bottom line. If there are problems with it, they can have complex ramifications, so we have to consider it carefully. This section is concerned with what is assessed, and the next one (24) with how.

- What is being assessed?
- Are the criteria laid down or are you free to change them?
- Are the assessment criteria consistent with the course aims?
- Do staff agree on the assessment criteria and the relative emphasis placed on them?
- Are they consistently applied?
- Are students clear about what the assessors want?
- Is there any evidence that students misperceive or misunderstand the criteria?

Assessment involves gathering evidence and making judgements about what students have learned. It is useful to bear this legal parallel in mind because, as in the courts, things can go wrong with the process in either way. Because it would take too long to gather evidence about every part of the course, assessment is always based on a sample of what has been done. This sample has to represent not only what was covered (ie, the topics or content) but the kind of learning involved (knowledge, application, analysis, understanding, etc). One might thus choose the right topic (origins of the First World War) but ask the wrong kind of question (*list* or *describe* rather than *analyse* or *compare*). And as in court, one also has to be careful about the way this evidence is obtained in terms of the appropriate methods and conditions (see the next section).

However, all this still leaves the underlying question: evidence of what? What has to be present in (or absent from) the evidence for it to be judged satisfactory or not? What is one looking for? What template does one have in mind in forming an opinion? This sends one back to the basic aims of the course. Rationally, we should know what it is we are trying to do when we teach and the widespread current emphasis on learning objectives and outcomes reflects that assumption (see Sections 2 and 13). The assessment criteria of many courses are straightforward, explicit, shared and agreed. But life is not always so simple. To begin with, some of the more generic or higher-order aims of education (capacity to analyse data, present arguments, evaluate evidence, grasp concepts, solve problems or think critically, for example) are by their very nature open-ended and difficult to pin down. We can hardly abandon such goals just because they are complex to assess. Second, there are often tacit as well as explicit elements in bodies of knowledge and practice that are not articulated and are therefore hard to get at through assessment. Third, the course may evolve as it goes along, sometimes responding to student needs or the natural dynamics of teaching, and develop in ways that shift or go beyond the original aims. Fourth, because education is often concerned with meanings, it is inherently open to differences of interpretation and individual staff may each have their own particular 'take' on what the course is about. (Most people will subscribe to a list of general aims; arguments arise over priorities and the devil is in the detail). Such differences may not become apparent until they surface in some disagreement about marking. Finally, the students will all have their own perception of what they are doing, which may or may not coincide with what the staff see as important.

Ensuring that assessment is 'valid' – that it tests what it should test – is by no means the simple or transparent matter that it is sometimes believed to be. Moreover, changes in assessment may have 'backwash' effects on teaching and learning, particularly in terms of the students' approach and attitude to learning. Where the assessment is carried out externally, there is the added problem of trying to interpret what the examiners are after, given not only their explicit statements about marking, but their actual track record in previous years. This problem is renewed every time the curriculum is changed, which these days happens frequently.

WHAT'S THE PROBLEM?

As noted right at the beginning of the book (see page 7), assessment is one of the critical aspects of the control of teaching, and the way you respond to this section will reflect that. Broadly speaking, the spectrum of internal to external control runs from adult education (where there may be no formal assessment anyway) through higher and further education to schools, but there are considerable differences within each sector. For example professional subjects in higher education such as medicine, law and engineering (not to mention teaching) are subject to greater external regulation than more purely academic subjects such as mathematics, languages or history. You may thus be limited in what you can do, but here are some possibilities:

- If the course is externally or nationally assessed, go to any work-shops or conferences that may help throw light on the criteria, especially if the course or its assessment has recently changed. You may well pick up some of the more tacit aspects of assessment that are not spelled out in the formal documentation.
- While any of your own staff who are involved in external or national marking will obviously be bound by strict rules of confid-entiality, they may nevertheless be able to give colleagues some general insights into the criteria.
- Analyse your own assessments against the stated aims and object-ives of the course. Look out for any lack of congruence in terms of both the topics and types of question. Pay particular attention to the key verbs in questions (*list, describe, discuss,* etc) to ensure that they are testing the appropriate type or level of learning.
- Get several staff to blind mark the same piece of work and discuss the results. You can do this for calculations as well as verbal work.
- As an experiment, blind mark the same piece of work again after an interval of six months or a year, to see if your judgement has changed over time.
- Get students to blind mark an anonymous or fictitious piece of work and discuss the results, focusing on the implicit criteria they use.
- Run any questions you set past a colleague or external examiner to check that they are really getting at what you want to assess. (You may have to do this anyway.)
- Explore the use of marking schemes that spell out the criteria for each category or band of marks. If these are already in place, go through them with the students; you cannot assume that they will automatically interpret them in the way you expect. General specifications are not enough; people need concrete examples of how it works out in practice.

We can take it for granted that this section will involve assessment, but what about the other headings in the COSTAS list?

A

SOLUTIONS

This and the next section on the methods and procedures of assessment should be taken together, and you may need to refer from one to the other, particularly in terms of problems you identify.

24 ARE THE ASSESSMENT METHODS AND PROCEDURES SATISFACTORY?

NO ☐ **?** ☐ **YES** ☐

Even if one has identified *what* one wants to assess (the criteria) one still has to work out *how* (methods and procedures). In the past, certain methods of assessment tended to be the norm in particular subjects or types of education: the skills test, the lab report and the unseen written exam reigned unquestioned in their own domains. Now the approach is more eclectic and we often use a mix of methods in any one field. This represents a less hidebound approach but equally raises the question: Are these the appropriate methods, singly or together? Merely using a combination of methods – as is sometimes recommended – does not in itself guarantee that the assessment will be better. And, even if the methods are appropriate, are they being used in the best way? How is the information that they yield processed in terms of marking, interpretation or judgements? Assessment can be troublesome in any of these ways and given its importance we need to be constantly alert to problems and looking for ways of refining and improving it (see Notes).

- What are the main assessment methods used on the course?
- How appropriate are they?
- How reliable are they?
- Do the students accept them?
- Do students have the skills necessary to undergo them?
- Are they seen as legitimate by external stakeholders?
- Are you and your colleagues competent to use them?
- Is the process of marking and grading satisfactory?
- Are the judgements presented in an appropriate way?

The list of possible assessment methods is now very long: true/false tests, completion tests, substitution tests, application tests, multiple-choice questions, problem tasks, short answer questions, unseen written exams, seen exams, open-book exams, essays, long essays, reports, individual projects, group projects, portfolios, in-tray exercises, simulation tests, practical tests, performance tests, placement reports, individual presentations, group presentations, oral exams, vivas. . . and on top of all these, specialized fields such as medicine and the performing arts have also developed their own particular methods.

This range of choice is fine but it does complicate things. One has to consider a number of factors in selecting a method. It might be valid (ie, test what you want to test) but be rather unreliable (yielding different results depending on the assessor, assessment conditions, or assessment centre). It might be complex and expensive to organize; this can be the case with methods that attempt to capture or reproduce real-life situations in vocational or professional fields. It might take a long time to construct and validate, as do multiple-choice tests, or a long time to mark, which is the problem with essays. It may get out of proportion and swallow up too much of the student's time, affecting other forms of assessment: this can happen with creative exercises. Where it involves work over a period of months, as projects often do, the goalposts may move over time.

There are other more subtle problems. Does one piece of assessment subsume other, simpler forms of test within itself? For example, can you rely on an essay-type answer that is mainly concerned with argument and analysis also to test the factual basis for these, or do you need to assess that knowledge separately? Most courses have different clusters and levels of objectives; do you test each on its own, or do you set comprehensive or synoptic assessments? Do the students know how to approach the test? If they do, might they become 'test-wise' in the sense of developing strategies to deal with the situation, and if so how does that affect the results? Do the students regard it as a valid assessment of what they have really learned or merely as a hoop through which they have to jump?

There are questions for staff also. How competent are they to carry out this form of assessment? Do they know how to frame questions, organize tests or papers, allocate time and set up the test environment? Above all, do they know what to do with the students' responses in terms of marking and making judgements? Are they operating on a criterion-referenced, norm-referenced or self-referenced basis, or on some mixture of these? Is everyone marking on the same basis? How good are the procedures and processes, and what happens if something goes wrong? What mechanisms are there for considering appeals or rectifying errors?

The degree of control that teachers or lecturers have over assessment varies enormously and will affect the way you respond to this section. Where assessment is determined and carried out externally, your scope will be limited to ensuring that both staff and students understand the process as well as possible. Where you and your colleagues have partial or total responsibility for assessment there is much more you can do, but also many more questions to ask.

Q | **WHAT'S THE PROBLEM?**

As noted above, the issue of control or regulation looms large and there may be severe limitations on the kinds of solutions you can consider. Be that as it may, here are some ideas to think about:

- Assessment is a specialized and sometimes technical field, so it may be useful to have one member of staff (you?) develop special expertise in it so that he or she can advise colleagues.
- Review your assessment process periodically. Ask not simply whether it is working well but whether it could work better, perhaps by employing different methods or procedures. Also, ensure that the process is properly documented. This is one aspect of teaching where procedures are crucial.
- Make sure that students know the rules of the game. If they are not already familiar with these, expose them to similar test conditions before they do the real thing.

- Each method of assessment makes particular kinds of demands and requires particular skills on the part of the student. For example, some tests involve oral skills, others written; some are timed, others untimed. In some, one needs to check for silly slips or errors, while in others there are rules and conventions about presentation. Unless such skills are seen as an intrinsic part of the test (a dubious argument), students should be alerted to them and prepared for them.
- Include questions on assessment in student evaluations or feedback forms in order to get the students' view. After all, it is they who have to undergo it.
- New staff need training on assessment; having gone through it themselves at some time in the past is not sufficient preparation. Organize workshops or a mentoring system whereby more experienced staff help the novices. Use double-marking as a training exercise.
- Introduce standard marking schemes if you think these will help to make the process more valid and reliable, but be aware that they can also make it less flexible and responsive and focus students' attention only on what is made explicit.
- Work out the amount of staff time each form of assessment takes from start to finish (initial discussion, preparation and setting, administering, marking, examiners' meetings, etc). This will give you a better handle on the organizational aspects of the process.
- Before you introduce any new method, find out how it has worked elsewhere. Check the literature or ask friends. Usually someone somewhere will have tried it already.
- Make use of external examiners if you have them. As well as adjudicating in particular cases, they can make helpful general comments on the assessment process, and indeed are usually required to do so. But they need to be involved at each stage in the process, not just at the final meeting, if they are really to understand it.
- Distinguish between feedback and assessment. Assessment gives feedback, but feedback need not always involve formal assessment. Ensure that students have opportunities to try things out, take risks and explore their learning without it always counting towards their results.
- Think carefully about how the results of assessment are communicated to students. Do they get an aggregate mark or is that

broken down into components or a profile? Is there any accompanying feedback? Is the process impersonal or personal? Is there any follow up? What are the next steps? Assessment, at the end of the day, should be an aspect of teaching, not the other way round.

Cost? Organization? Staff? Time? Students?

SOLUTIONS

25 ARE THE RESULTS AS GOOD AS EXPECTED?

NO ☐   ? ☐   YES ☐

This is one of two final 'catch-all' questions about the course. In one way, results provide the most obvious indicator of the success of a course, and likewise the most obvious indication of problems or trouble. However, it is not always easy to know what results should be attributed to: Good or poor selection of students? Good or poor motivation? A good or poor learning environment? Good or poor teaching? One teacher or another? Appropriate or inappropriate assessment? Rising or falling standards? The question also raises the issue of expectations. What do you count as 'good'? Are your expectations too low? Are they unreasonably high? Have you settled into a certain set of assumptions – perhaps even self-fulfilling prophecies – that relate to certain types or groups of students? And what do the students expect of themselves? It is not possible to suggest all the ramifications of this question here. Only you can explore it, analysing the pattern of results (perhaps over time and across institutions) and if necessary tracing the diagnosis back to some of the issues raised in previous sections in this and the first chapter. Likewise, only you can come up with potential solutions in the light of that analysis, solutions that may relate not just to one but to several aspects of the work. If your course is not formally assessed at all, you will need to identify some other measure of performance or achievement that you can use instead.

WHAT'S THE PROBLEM?

What, if anything, can you do about this? Remember COSTAS.

SOLUTIONS

26 WAS THE COURSE A POSITIVE EXPERIENCE FOR EVERYONE?

NO ☐   ? ☐   YES ☐

Although results are often seen as the ultimate measure of a course, there is one further general aspect that needs to be considered. Teaching and learning are not easy. By definition, they are trying to press forward into some state or condition that did not exist previously: knowing or understanding something that one did not know or grasp before, being able to do something that one could not do in the past, becoming aware of something that hitherto was unconscious or hidden from one. Experiencing and bringing about such changes can be a real challenge for both parties. But it should still be a positive experience, one that (at a minimum) people do not regret, that hopefully leaves them further on in some perhaps indefinable way, and with an appetite for more. When they finish a course, students may decide that they do not want to pursue that particular subject any further, but they should not feel that it was a waste of time, or have been alienated by it or wish never to set eyes on the teacher again.

This question, however, concerns everyone, and that includes you. In our preoccupation with student motivation, attitudes and approaches to learning we should not forget that teaching, for all its stresses and difficulties, should also be a positive experience, something worthwhile. If it is not, teachers begin to withdraw from their work, taking refuge in cynicism, detachment or routine, or eventually leaving the profession altogether. So, how was the course?

WHAT'S THE PROBLEM?

Any answers? And do not forget COSTAS.

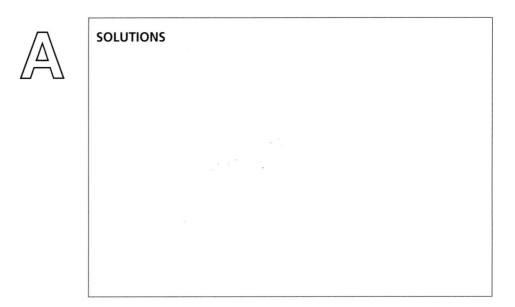

SOLUTIONS

Anything else?

This completes Chapter 2 on 'Trouble-shooting the course', but before you fill in the summary profile think about whether there are any other issues you want to identify.

> **WHAT'S THE PROBLEM?**

Now consider possible solutions and run them past the standard checklist.

> **SOLUTIONS**

Profile

As with Chapter 1, you should now complete the summary profile for this chapter. This will help you to get an overview of the course and give you something that you can think about or share with your colleagues. Remember that your initial three-point response (NO / ? / YES) now needs to be translated into a seven-point scale (NO = 1 or 2; ? = 3, 4 or 5; YES = 6 or 7).

	No	?	Yes
12. Are the students on the right course?	1 2	3 4 5	6 7
13. Do they know what to expect?	1 2	3 4 5	6 7
14. Have they got the resources for learning?	1 2	3 4 5	6 7
15. Is the course manageable?	1 2	3 4 5	6 7
16. Is the course well delivered?	1 2	3 4 5	6 7
17. Do the students know how to go about their studies?	1 2	3 4 5	6 7
18. Are the teachers good models?	1 2	3 4 5	6 7
19. Do the students get the support they need?	1 2	3 4 5	6 7
20. Do the students learn from one another?	1 2	3 4 5	6 7
21. Is there a good learning environment?	1 2	3 4 5	6 7
22. Is education valued in the wider community?	1 2	3 4 5	6 7
23. Are the assessment criteria satisfactory?	1 2	3 4 5	6 7
24. Are the assessment methods and procedures satisfactory?	1 2	3 4 5	6 7
25. Are the results as good as expected?	1 2	3 4 5	6 7
26. Was the course a positive experience for everyone?	1 2	3 4 5	6 7
Anything else?	1 2	3 4 5	6 7

Action plan

Note down the main actions you intend to take in response to the problems you have identified at the level of the course. Specify the general aim, the specific actions and stages that you plan, the person or persons responsible (including yourself) and the expected time frame. Since, as implied by the COSTAS checklist, changes at this level can have various consequences and ramifications, you might like to make a note of likely barriers or pitfalls as well.

AIM	ACTION	PERSON	DEADLINE

3 Managing it all

Introduction

At first sight, it may seem strange to have a chapter on management in a book about teaching, and if you see yourself primarily as a lecturer or teacher you may assume that it does not apply to you. However, there are good reasons for including such a chapter and for reading it.

Management is a relatively new concept in education. In the past, there was teaching and there was administration. The former comprised curriculum and pedagogy; the purpose of the latter was to underpin them both in as smooth and unobtrusive a way as possible. The arrival of 'management' in education reflects the more general spread of the topic, which now reaches into every nook and cranny of public and private life. Not only do we manage commercial enterprises and public services but our own health, finances, relationships and even emotions. In this broad sense, management exists wherever there are complex choices and decisions to be made.

There are also particular reasons for its penetration of education. Whereas in the past courses and programmes could be relatively stable for long periods, now they seem to be in a continual state of change. Patterns of assessment and the structure of qualifications are regularly modified. Teaching itself keeps changing, partly because of the impact of new technology. All this development has to be managed. Then there is the growing emphasis on accountability and value for money; no longer is the curriculum a 'secret garden', the jealously guarded preserve of professional expertise. The individual autonomy of the lecturer or teacher has been modified by the need to work in teams, and qualified by reference to external bodies and stakeholders. The baronial and sometimes arbitrary powers that heads of departments and institutions often had in the past are now subject to democratic or consultative processes. Students are seen less as objects of instruction, more as partners in learning. In short, we can no longer look at teaching in isolation.

That said, the managerial revolution in education (as in other public services) has not been an entirely happy or positive experience. The critique of 'managerialism' taps multiple roots, but in broad terms signals a distrust of and alienation from some of the values and procedures that have come along with the new arrival. This chapter does not set out to give either an exposition or critique of educational management but simply to explore, in a more pragmatic way, a range of organizational issues that can affect teaching. It is based on a particular model of management that is of course open to argument (see Notes). It is concerned with managing as a *process* rather than management as a *designated cadre*. As has already been pointed out in Section 15, students need to manage their learning. Teachers, likewise, have to manage their classes. Beyond that, the extent to which you manage your teaching will depend on the kind of institution you work in – whether it is relatively hierarchical or collegial – and your position in it. In all institutions, there will be a superstructure of middle and senior management, but the answer to the question 'Who is the manager?' may in many cases be 'You'. And even if your job is limited to classroom teaching, it is important that you understand something of the structures and pressures that shape your work.

As with the rest of the book, the view of management implied here is a relatively contingent one. The answer to most questions about managing, as about teaching, is: 'It depends'. Given the enormous range and variety of educational institutions, this makes it particularly difficult to suggest likely solutions, hence that part of each section is shorter and more generalized than in previous chapters, and you will need to use your own common sense and judgement in coming up with possible answers. Moreover, there may not be an answer. Management problems, like teaching ones, sometimes take the form of a dilemma where one is trying to achieve the best available compromise or trade-off rather than some optimal solution. Thus the need for change (a favourite management topic) has to be balanced with the need for stability (which one hears less about). The emphasis on planning (which is now pervasive at all levels) has to be balanced against the advantages of improvisation and incrementalism (see Notes), and tempered with the recognition that teachers are often reacting rather than acting. One of the illusions peddled by some management writing is that we are always in control. Often, we are not.

Working through the chapter

You should continue to follow the same steps as in the previous chapters in working through each section (if necessary, refer back to pages 4–5 in the Introduction).

The pattern of sections changes slightly, reflecting the fact that we are now talking about things that have a more indirect relationship with or impact on teaching. There is therefore an additional response box for the 'Effect on teaching' (and, by extension, learning). Some of the possible solutions will lie within your power, others may go beyond it. You can still use the COSTAS checklist (see pages 69–70), though you will probably find that the two final headings (*Assessment* and *Students*) become less salient, because the impact of management on them is less direct.

When you have completed the chapter (and thus the book), it may be useful for you to map out, on a separate sheet of paper, any clusters or sets of problems that seem to straddle all three chapters. This will help you to see the relationship between different levels of problem (session, course, management) as well as different types, and should form a useful tool for reflection and discussion.

27 ARE THINGS WELL ORGANIZED?

NO ☐   ? ☐   YES ☐

This question covers everything from the day-to-day running of a course or department to the wider issues of organizational structure and process. At the most concrete level, it is concerned with whether things get done in the right way and at the right time or whether, by contrast, they slip through the net, fall between the cracks, or get delayed or even forgotten. The importance of this everyday organization should not be underestimated; it forms the basic working environment for both staff and students. At its best, it seems smooth and efficient to the point where it is virtually invisible; at worst, it makes life difficult in a hundred little ways that sap energy, divert attention and lead to a slow build-up of frustration. But organizational issues go beyond the practical or everyday. The essential problem is that organizations have to break down what they do into specific roles and tasks, but equally have to put them all together again in a coherent, working whole. They have to both allocate and coordinate. Problems can arise with either of these functions and beyond such issues of structure and function there is the more elusive question of the organizational culture, ethos or style, and whether it reinforces or undermines what people do both individually and collectively.

- Do staff know what they are expected to do?
- Do they feel able to do what is expected of them?
- Do staff identify with their roles?
- Are the lines of communication clear?
- Is the organizational structure appropriate?
- Are things properly coordinated?
- Are problems followed up?
- Are there frequent hiccups or cock-ups?
- Are there any weak links individually or organizationally?

Organizational problems can arise for a number of reasons. The first is that people are not sure what they are meant to be doing. If there is a basic lack of clarity about roles, responsibilities and tasks, it can lead to organizational gaps (nobody does it) or overlaps (several people do it, perhaps differently). It can also generate a good deal of conflict between staff over the longer term. Even if roles and tasks are reasonably well defined, there may be poor communication between individuals or units. This may be due simply to a bad flow of information, or it may sometimes reflect internal boundaries and territoriality (see Notes). Educational institutions are highly demarcated in terms of subjects and departments, and this means that lateral communication and interaction can be difficult. Also, some individuals have a tendency to hoard information and keep it to themselves; after all, information is power.

The answer to these difficulties might seem to be better coordination but this often runs into a different, 'vertical' problem. Because of their traditions and the nature of their work, educational institutions comprise, as noted in the Introduction, a complex mixture of hierarchy and collegiality. On the one hand, there is a formal structure of top-down decision making. On the other, most of the expertise and activity lies at the base of the organizational pyramid, so teachers and lecturers see their work in terms of autonomous collegiality: they know best what to do in their own particular patch.

There is a similar ambiguity about procedures. In recent years, there have been determined attempts, at both national and institutional levels, to clarify and tighten up on procedures to do with admissions, curricula, teaching, assessment and so on. These have certainly helped improve record-keeping, standardize practice and ensure follow-up. However, the rational ideal of clear structures and transparent processes runs into the basic problem that education has strong tacit or informal elements as well as explicit formal ones, perhaps because it is essentially concerned with people and meanings. Procedures do not really work unless people believe in them, and staff, being clever folk, can often find ways round them if they want to.

Finally, some teachers have an ingrained dislike of 'admin', regarding it as boring, routine and a distraction from their proper task. That distaste can harden into an organizational gap between teaching staff on the one hand and administrative and secretarial staff on the other that affects liaison between them. Education is administratively complex because it deals with so many 'products' (courses, programmes) and so many 'clients' (students, stakeholders). Relating the professional and administrative aspects is thus often a problem.

Education is thus complex and often messy in organizational terms, and the attempts over the last couple of decades to 'manage' it better have produced equal and opposite reactions against 'managerialism', 'bureaucracy' and 'paperwork'. That is, however, no excuse for not doing the job well; the task is to find a way of managing the organization that will, in the end, facilitate teaching and learning. That implies a more contextualized notion of management than has sometimes been the case hitherto.

WHAT'S THE PROBLEM?

EFFECT ON TEACHING?

Given the diversity of institutions and their situations, it is difficult to do more than suggest a number of general solutions, which may or may not be relevant. A lot will depend also on your role and position within the institution, and how wide or senior your responsibilities are. Consider the following, but you may also be able to come up with something of your own that is right for your particular situation and institution.

- Look carefully at people's existing job specifications in relation both to the organization's tasks and to one another. Be aware that any changes may have contractual implications, if only in terms of custom and practice.
- If they do not already exist, devise organizational maps, flow-charts and calendars. The first allow people to see where they fit in, the second what stage of the cycle they are at, and the third to work and think ahead. These can be useful not only at institutional but at departmental or even section level.
- Have shorter meetings more often, rather than longer, less frequent ones. That way you may be able to keep on top of things better. A week is a long time in teaching, as in politics.
- Try to ensure that staff have occasions to meet informally, for example over coffee, lunch and tea, or after work. Such opportunities seem to have declined in recent years with the general increase in workload, and individual timetables also make it difficult to meet one's colleagues. Such contacts help staff keep abreast of the work and may allow them to catch problems at an early stage before they develop.
- Involve admin/secretarial staff in key meetings. They often have their ear to the ground and (to mix the metaphor) need to be kept in the picture.
- Create a comments/suggestions box for both staff and students.
- Simplify procedures and reduce paperwork wherever possible, but take account of the need for formal record-keeping where necessary.
- Trust people. Explain to them clearly what is needed, check after a while that they are doing the job, and then let them get on with it. But be available to give advice on exceptional, new or awkward problems.
- Do not reorganize endlessly. Give things a chance to work and give people a chance to settle down.
- Apply Occam's Razor to the organization. Do not adopt a complicated procedure where a simpler one will do.

Most of these suggestions relate to staff and organization in the COSTAS checklist. Some will take time, but may equally save time in the longer run.

SOLUTIONS

28 ARE PROBLEMS DEALT WITH QUICKLY?

NO ☐ **?** ☐ **YES** ☐

Murphy's Law states that if a thing can go wrong, it will. Even in the best-organized department or programme, problems or crises can blow up suddenly like a squall at sea, taking everyone by surprise. This is partly because of the inherent complexity of teaching, described in the previous section; it is difficult to be aware of everything that is happening and what everyone is feeling. It is also because of the basic unpredictability of a process that is by definition about change (ie, learning) and that involves people negotiating meanings and relationships with one another in a charged environment. Not for nothing has teaching been described as a 'hot' activity (see Notes). Then there is the impact of external changes in funding, regulations, curricula and qualifications, some of which are rapid and difficult to foresee. Crises are thus fairly normal; what matters is how you and the department or institution respond to them.

- What kinds of problems or crises occur at departmental or pro-gramme level?
- What kinds of crises occur at institutional level?
- Do they tend to happen at particular times of year?
- Are they associated with particular types of student, subject or staff?
- Are they typically triggered by events within the institution or beyond it?
- With hindsight, could anyone have seen them coming?
- Does the department/institution learn from them?

The language of management is full of the discourse of rational planning and control: goals, strategies, executive decisions, implementation and the like. It is also rich in the metaphors of chaos and confusion: things going pear-shaped, being caught on the wrong foot, off guard, on the hop and so on. It is not surprising therefore that there is a whole literature devoted to crisis management, or more colloquially 'fire-fighting'. Managers have to plan, but they also have to be able to respond. The process is both proactive and reactive, and people or organizations that do not react effectively can lose a lot of credibility very quickly indeed.

In order to respond, the organization must be aware that there is something wrong or going wrong in the first place, and this is often the first problem: it may lack the sensors to pick it up and give early warning of it. In human terms, this comes down to the staff, who may be too remote, preoccupied or simply too busy to notice. Organizational and structural change create their own kind of 'noise' in the system that makes it more difficult to detect signals of this kind. When the organization does become aware, it may be too cumbersome and bureaucratic to do anything; it remains in thrall to its own rules and procedures and thus incapable of handling anything out of the ordinary. Well-established and prestigious organizations are particularly prone to this kind of rigidity. Even if the structures do not prevent a response, individuals may engage in buck-passing, something that the relative fuzziness of some educational organizations (everyone is vaguely responsible for everything) makes easy. Or the problem may become a point of conflict between two parts of the organization that have vested interests in resolving (or not resolving) the matter in a particular way. Or there may just seem to be a general paralysis. No one takes charge.

Organizations can take their eye off the ball for better or at least more understandable reasons. To begin with, there may be rather a lot of balls, given the constant stream of official initiatives and the general state of change that most teachers have to cope with nowadays. Staff may be so preoccupied with bigger issues (finance, new regulations, numbers) that they miss the smaller signs. Worsening staff–student ratios make it more difficult for teachers to know their students individually, and modular systems can diffuse or continually re-shuffle staff–student relationships and the personal knowledge that goes with them. Rapid turnover of staff can also weaken communication among teachers in a similar way. They may not know who to go to about a problem or, even if they do, not know them well enough to broach what may be a ticklish or sensitive issue.

WHAT'S THE PROBLEM?

EFFECT ON TEACHING?

As with the previous section, the solutions you propose will depend very much on the nature of the problem and on your own position within the organization. You may want to focus on issues either at the departmental or institutional level. There are two broad kinds of response. The first is structural. This involves reviewing and changing the structures and procedures of the department or institution so that it becomes capable of responding rapidly and effectively to problems as they arise. This in turn may involve some clarification of staff roles; where does the buck stop? Second, there is the human element. The problem may lie rather in a lack of communication or breakdown of relationships. You may therefore need to improve the quality of the contact among staff or between staff and students. Informal as well as formal communication may be important in this.

You should also try to ensure that you learn from past mistakes. It is important to review cases where things have gone off the rails. Treat them to a formal 'clinical audit' (as in medicine) by asking one member of staff to assemble the evidence and lead a structured discussion of it. That should help not only to bring out the key features of the case but also to take some of the heat out of it. Try to work towards a blame-free culture that will encourage staff to report rather than conceal problems. Many faults are systemic rather than individual, or down to individuals operating in a dysfunctional systemic context. You may also find it useful to look at how other kinds of organizations outside education address issues of error and blame. One factor influencing all organizations nowadays is the increased possibility of related litigation, which unfortunately can lead to 'defensive practice'.

In terms of COSTAS, the main implications of such ideas seem to be for staff and the organization, though time may be a factor also.

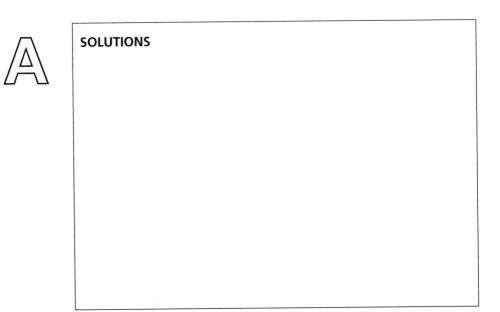

SOLUTIONS

29   IS THERE ADEQUATE PLANNING?

NO ☐   ? ☐   YES ☐

Planning has become such a familiar part of the work of teachers that it is difficult now to imagine life without it. We have lesson plans, course plans, programme plans, departmental and institutional plans, annual plans, rolling plans, five-year plans, personal development plans, succession plans. . . Teachers have always had to think and work ahead to some extent, but the contemporary emphasis on systematic planning is more recent, and stems ultimately from a rational paradigm of teaching and management. That paradigm is questioned by those who believe in a more incremental or pragmatic approach or who think that the apparent rationality in fact masks a more political (small p) process (see Notes). It is important therefore to stand back a little from the idea of planning and ask why it is currently so central to teaching and whether it actually works. The question is thus not whether there is planning but whether there is enough planning and of the right sort. As with the previous section, you may want to focus on issues at a particular level in the organization.

- How much change is there from one cycle/year to the next?
- What is your time horizon? How far can you realistically see ahead?
- Is there an effective planning system?
- Do certain individuals/units hold everyone else up?
- Are there any recent cases where plans have had to be abandoned because of unforeseen developments?
- Are there any recent examples of hasty decisions?
- Does everyone take planning seriously?
- Do you feel you are ahead of the game or always trying to catch up?

Planning assumes change. If there were no change we could just continue in our own sweet way and not need to think ahead. But the notion of planning also assumes that such change can to some extent be foreseen. It is predicated on the idea that we can have some kind of knowledge of the future, through projection or prediction. It also assumes that we can do something now to prepare: that we can take steps that will enable us to meet or realize that future when the time comes. If these three conditions are not met, there is no point in planning.

In reality, the situation may be more ambiguous. The changes may be major or minor. The first kind will require some planning, but we may be able to deal with the second by adapting as we go along. Thus, as noted in Chapter 1, teaching a class may be a subtle blend of planning and improvisation, staff may make running changes to a course or programme as it is in progress, and a head of department may vire funding in order to cope with a sudden need. In each case, any plan that there is will act as a general framework or outline within which more immediate, localized decisions may be made.

A different problem arises from the fact that educational organizations have to respond to both internal and external factors. On the one hand, there may be changes in the pattern of staffing, the progression of students or the structure of departments. But many of the changes impacting on teaching come from the outside: shifts in student demand, changes in the level or conditions of funding, new regulations governing courses or assessment, and government or official initiatives of various kinds. An institution that is relatively stable internally may yet be blown off course by some external development that was difficult to predict.

For all the difficulties involved in planning in education, it remains important for two reasons. The first is the long lead time needed to put in place many changes. Teaching is not an area where things can be done overnight, and it can take months or even years to bring together the right combination of financial, human and physical resources to accomplish the job. The second reason is that, as seen in Section 27, teaching is inherently complex. It is a composite activity involving a number of different elements, not only in terms of staffing, structures, materials and facilities, but also the different aspects of courses: initial admission or selection, teaching and learning, individual support and guidance, and assessment. We need to plan in order to ensure that all the parts come together as they should.

Planning failure is typically of four kinds. There may be little or no attempt to plan ahead in the first place; staff may be complacent, parochial, short-sighted or simply too preoccupied with staying afloat to engage in the necessary thinking. Plans may also fail because they are unrealistic or inadequately grounded in the available evidence and data. Third, they may be too rigid and fall apart when confronted by the first major hurdle; there may be no 'Plan B' or contingency planning. Finally, a plan may fail because it does not carry the staff with it. Although with the growth of central bureaucratic regulation, teachers may appear to exercise less control over their work than they used to, in fact they still retain a good deal of discretionary power at the chalkface.

WHAT'S THE PROBLEM?

EFFECT ON TEACHING?

As with other sections in this chapter on the management of teaching, the breadth of the issues makes it difficult to suggest specific solutions here. Most of the relevant points are implicit in the preceding analysis. First, one needs to decide whether the basic conditions of planning are met, or whether a more incremental, opportunistic or pragmatic approach might not be better. Planning is not necessarily the appropriate approach, and one should not assume that it is always a good thing. Where there is a substantial degree of uncertainty, it is a good idea to sketch out alternative scenarios before deciding which is the most viable, but even then to have fall-back or alternative strategies.

If there is a distinct pattern or rhythm of activities, for example semester-length courses, an academic year or a quinquennial departmental review, that points to a regular planning cycle that everyone should be familiar with. The resource implications of plans need to be carefully considered, not just in terms of the up-front investment but the sometimes less obvious running costs. Some of the detailed preparation on specific aspects of a plan can often be done by subgroups who will report back; that usually helps develop specialist expertise and saves everyone else's time. However, it is important to involve or consult the people who will eventually be carrying out the plan, since they need to feel ownership of and be committed to it. Finally, early warning is an important aspect of planning, so it is important to have people with their ear to the ground or on the inside track who can alert you to what is being proposed. That way you can move quickly when the moment comes. It is also worth noting that planning is intimately related to the next section on evaluation (30) and also the later one on leadership (34).

Your proposed solutions will depend on what level you are operating at: section, subject, department, year, faculty or the institution as a whole. Having said that, you may find that these different levels interlock in various ways and that even if you want to focus on subject or departmental issues, there are wider factors that 'frame' your decisions.

A

SOLUTIONS

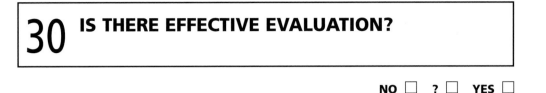

30 IS THERE EFFECTIVE EVALUATION?

NO ☐   ? ☐   YES ☐

There are three words in education that refer to the gathering of evidence and making of judgements: assessment, which usually refers to students, and which was explored in Sections 23 and 24; appraisal, which usually applies to staff; and evaluation, which usually relates to courses and teaching. This section is concerned with the last. Even if a course ran only once, it would be important purely for professional reasons to evaluate it and see how successful it had been. However, education is typically a repetitive activity in which courses run again and again and often come round in a regular cycle. This makes it all the more important to find out what happened during one course so that any lessons can be learned for subsequent ones. The most obvious indication of this is the results. As was pointed out in Section 25, however, it is not always easy to know what led to success or failure, or to what causes effects should be attributed. This means that one needs to probe further into the processes and interstices of the course: the aims, the curriculum, the materials, the teaching and learning, the environment, indeed many of the questions posed in this book. Having gathered such information one has to analyse and synthesize it in some judgement or set of judgements about what happened. Such judgements can then be fed into decisions about the next course. Thus the loop is closed.

- Are courses evaluated formally or informally?
- What are the criteria of evaluation?
- What are the methods of evaluation?
- Do staff take evaluation seriously?
- Do the students take it seriously?
- What is done with the results?

The concept of quality has loomed large in education in recent years and even become institutionalized in the titles of official bodies. One problem with 'quality' is that, rather like happiness, it is extremely difficult to define, to the point where some people argue that (again like happiness) it can only be recognized, not described. Moreover, its original sense of the intrinsic nature of something (eg a proper cup of coffee) has given way to more extrinsic definitions such as 'fitness for purpose'. Because of these complexities, it may be more useful for us to focus on the process (evaluation) that leads to this elusive outcome. However, the quality debate has at least been useful in highlighting the fact that quality is a matter both of procedures and of attitudes. One without the other will not suffice, and the same is true of evaluation.

To begin with, one has to get the procedures right. This is no simple matter since it immediately raises (as with assessment) the criterion question: what point of reference, standard or benchmark are we using to judge the course? The simplest evaluation models match terminal outcomes against initial aims but there may also be important unplanned or unintended outcomes. Then there are the decisions about data collection: does one rely on student questionnaires, group discussions, staff reactions, participant or non-participant observation, or comments from external stakeholders such as employers? Lurking under these methodological questions are the deeper issues of the relationship between internal and external evaluation, the balance of explicit and tacit elements in teaching (including the hidden curriculum) and the problem of multiple realities: Does everyone experience the same course? Indeed, where does the course exist? And to what extent should the emphasis be on formative (interim) or summative (final) evaluation? The first allows one to make running changes while the teaching is still in progress; the second provides the overall judgement, at least for this round of the course.

Such questions have been worked over very thoroughly in the evaluation literature, but less attention has been paid to the other element, namely attitudes. Evaluation is only effective if people want it to be. Students need to take it seriously enough to give considered responses, and to feel that there is something in it for them or their successors; this means that they in turn need feedback on how their own feedback has been used. The problem for staff is more complex. As noted elsewhere, teaching requires both involvement (the bringing of one's person to it) and detachment (the capacity to stand back and reflect on it). Teaching can be seen both as 'me' and 'it'. The more routine, common and shared the practice of evaluation becomes, the more normal and perhaps acceptable such analysis seems. But that very routine also carries an organizational risk, which is that we get procedure for procedure's sake: the findings are not really internalized by staff and acted on by the department or institution. So there may be some rather tired, cursory or defensive discussion of evaluation reports in the course committee at the end of term, and that's that.

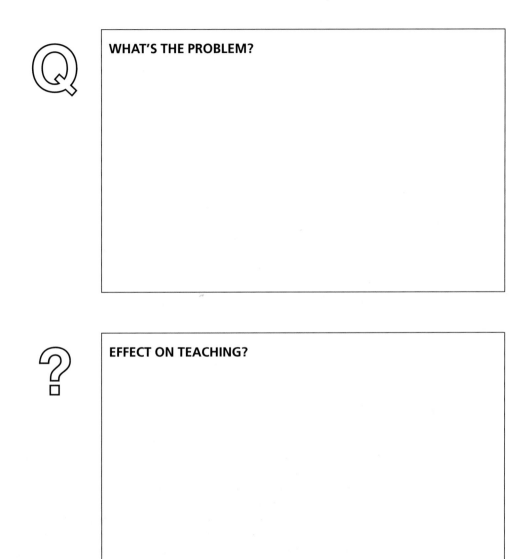

WHAT'S THE PROBLEM?

EFFECT ON TEACHING?

Here are some ideas to consider.

- Evaluation is a complex, technical topic, so if time and funds permit, it may be useful to have one member of staff develop special expertise in it so that he or she can advise colleagues.
- However formalized the process becomes, informal communication remains important. Try to ensure that staff have time to chat informally to students and to one another. This will allow them to get a feel for how the course is going and to pick up emerging problems more quickly.
- Develop a database of quantitative indicators (applications, admission trends, student data, module choice, dropout, results, first destinations, etc). This will allow you to monitor trends over time and across courses and help make relative sense of evaluation information.
- Discuss identification with teaching among staff. Explore how people regard the activity in terms of self-investment, self-efficacy, commitment, detachment, risk, success and so on. This may seem a long way from evaluation, but such attitudes and beliefs fundamentally influence people's perception of and approach to it.
- Apply the same principles to evaluation as you would to student assessment: be informative, constructive, supportive and suggest something to do, some way of moving forward.
- Do not place evaluation at the bottom of the committee agenda where it may only get limited discussion as people gather their files. Make it a priority; after all, what is more important than knowing how well you are doing?
- Education typically has long-term aims and short-term measures. If possible, try getting some follow-up evaluation of your provision from former students. By then they may have a better perspective on it.
- The evaluation of training is more complex than that of education because it needs to investigate not only what the trainees have learned, but how that learning has affected their performance, and how that performance has in turn affected the organization. The further one goes down this chain of effects, the more difficult it becomes to disentangle the impact of the training from everything else that may have affected the trainee's subsequent behaviour, for example pay rises, a change of manager, new equipment or altered procedures in the workplace. Likewise, problems with

the impact of training may stem from a lack of receptivity on the part of the organization or immediate colleagues rather than the training itself (see Notes).

Evaluation may have implications for all the COSTAS headings: cost, organization, staff, time, assessment and students. It is one of the most far-reaching aspects of the management of teaching.

A

SOLUTIONS

31   IS THERE SUFFICIENT STABILITY?

NO ☐   ? ☐   YES ☐

Organizations, like individuals, need a degree of stability in their lives. At the most basic level some measure of consistency and regularity is necessary for us to process information: we have to be able to recognize phenomena, discern patterns and establish relationships between things. Stability allows us to project ahead and make some assumptions about how the world is going to be tomorrow or next month. It also allows us to build up relationships with other people based on expected behaviours. It enables us to 'routinize' activities and decisions, so saving energy and freeing up our limited attention to deal with more complex or less predictable problems or situations; thus the experienced car driver can take the basic operations for granted while concentrating on the traffic conditions or chatting to his or her passenger. Stability also permits us, over a period of time, to refine and deepen our expertise through the constant repetition-with-minor-variations of procedures and processes. These rather theoretical arguments add up to a very practical point about teaching: is there enough stability to allow teachers to get on top of the job?

- What kinds of change affect your work in the classroom?
- What kinds of change affect your work in the organization?
- Do you feel comfortable with the rate of change?
- Are there any areas of your work that are relatively stable?
- Do the changes seem to come mainly from outside or inside the organization?
- How do you cope with change in your work?
- How do your colleagues?
- What support do you get?

The previous sections on organization, problem solving, planning and evaluation all involve certain assumptions about stability and change in teaching. The very idea of an organization implies some degree of permanence over and above the individuals who comprise it and who may join or leave; concepts such as 'organizational memory' and 'organizational learning' suggest that one can treat the organization as a continuing entity. As was noted in Section 29, planning likewise involves assumptions about continuity and change, and there would be little point in evaluating anything if teaching was completely discontinuous.

Stability can of course bring its own problems if individuals or departments get into so deep a rut that they cannot then change direction when necessary. It can create complacency and a gradual loss of the ability to imagine things otherwise, which leads to every new suggestion being ruled out as impossible and impractical. It can also induce boredom. But the problem nowadays is more likely to be the opposite: a constant stream of innovations to do with aims, curricula, teaching or assessment; rewriting of regulations; re-formulation of guidelines; re-structuring of departments or whole institutions; reframing of missions and priorities; all of which potentially destabilize both individuals and organizations. Add to these the continual stimulus of technological change and it is hardly surprising that it all seems too much sometimes.

The result is that staff can begin to suffer from innovation fatigue or simply feel bewildered or punch-drunk. They have just got to the point of bedding down one new activity or procedure when another one comes along. Or a change is introduced in one area of the work (eg, admissions) without reference to what is happening in another (eg, curriculum or assessment). This can have several consequences. One is that teaching itself comes to be seen increasingly in abstract, procedural terms, and the pedagogical heart goes out of the work. Just as students who are placed under excessive pressure to 'cover the ground' may regress from 'deep' to 'surface' learning, so teachers begin to engage in surface teaching, doing what they see as necessary to get through the week and satisfy the minimum requirements (see Note for page 31). Another consequence is that staff begin to withdraw psychologically from their work, a process that can lead to their eventually leaving the profession. Or else they learn to live in a split world, where the public, official version of teaching becomes increasingly remote from the private phenomenology. Or they just burn out.

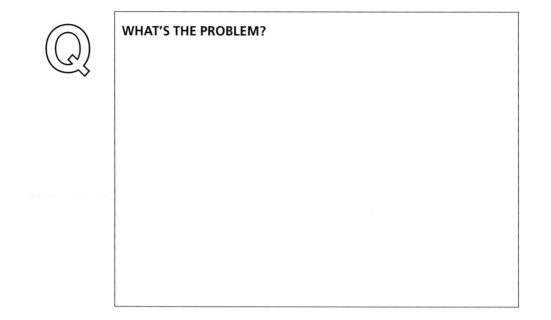

WHAT'S THE PROBLEM?

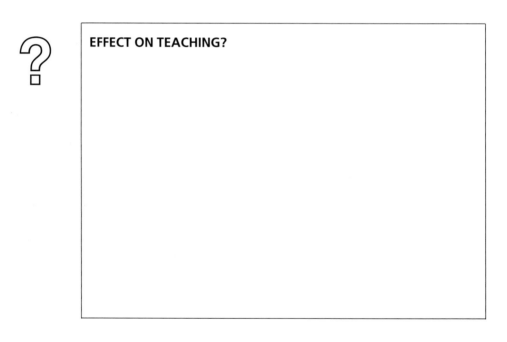

EFFECT ON TEACHING?

The causes of instability are often external and therefore may be largely out of your or your colleagues' control. It is difficult therefore to suggest practical solutions. However, you might find it useful to think about the following:

- Explain any changes to those involved so that they do not seem merely arbitrary or capricious. If you are on the receiving end, ask (at an appropriate opportunity) for such explanations.
- If you are responsible for decisions about change, do not adopt or impose unrealistic timescales; they will merely create resentment.
- Recognize that the process of change in itself exacts a certain cost in terms of time, attention and effort, regardless of the merits of the development. Try to quantify this cost in terms of staff time, and build it into your decision about whether to go ahead.
- If you are considering some change, find out first if it has worked elsewhere. If necessary, visit the place and talk to staff.
- Be alert to the knock-on or side-effects of any proposed innovation. Teaching is a highly interconnected activity and a change in one aspect will usually impact on others. (Murphy's Cousin's Law: solving one problem creates two others.)
- Consider the merits of a 'big-bang' change rather than a more gradual, incremental one. It may be easier to get it all over with at once, and then give people time to settle in to the new regime and make it work.
- When you introduce a change, decide how long you are going to let it run before you review it again.
- Evaluate any major changes that have been made after an appropriate lag. Try to ensure that the organization learns from them.
- There is a lot of knowledge and know-how embedded in any organization and this needs to be used. Tap the experience of staff who have been around for some time and who may have lived through changes.
- When you propose any change, consider what effect it will have on the social fabric and working relationships of the organization. As budgets show, people are the main resource of any educational institution and the human ecology can be quite delicate and easily damaged.

SOLUTIONS

This and the next section should be treated as a pair.

32 IS THERE ENOUGH DEVELOPMENT?

NO ☐   **?** ☐   **YES** ☐

The answers to this question and the previous one might seem like opposites: if there is not enough stability it might be because there is too much change and vice versa. However, development here means something slightly different from change *per se*: it refers to intentional or deliberate change, change that is to some degree managed or under control, as compared to the fire-fighting described in Section 28 or the necessary response to external initiatives discussed in the last. It is a truism to say that we live in an age of change, and education is not exempt from this; indeed, it actually contributes to it. Commercial organizations will often manage change by acquiring new companies or buying in new expertise, but educational institutions are usually limited in the extent to which they can do either. Takeovers or mergers are rare and staff turnover can be low. Schools, colleges and universities therefore have to rely primarily on internal development to meet new needs and exploit new opportunities. That development can in turn be subdivided into curriculum development, staff development and organization development. The question is: is there enough of each?

- Does the institution seem in touch/out of touch with current trends?
- Does it seem ill-/well-equipped to respond to current needs?
- Does your department?
- Is there enough emphasis on curriculum development?
- Do staff have the necessary expertise to cope with changes in teaching or assessment? Do you?
- Is staff development taken seriously?
- Is the organizational culture generally innovative or defensive?

The current emphasis on organized CPD (continuing professional development) in education is a welcome and overdue recognition of the fact that initial teacher training is now only the first chapter in a lifelong professional story. However, it also carries the risk that informal development is undervalued or ignored. Much of the learning that goes on in organizations takes place in and through the work itself, by confronting new tasks, utilizing informal networks, working together in teams, searching for information, scanning current material and even apparently casual activities such as staffroom chat. The first priority of any organization should therefore be to maximize such informal learning and create conditions in which it is recognized and used. This may come down to some very simple things like ensuring that staff have the time and place to talk, or giving individuals just that little bit of freedom or support that will allow them to develop some new materials or method of teaching. But more generally it means listening to staff and backing their initiatives, things that the organizational climate may or may not welcome. It also means inducting new staff carefully and providing them with the mentoring and support they need to cope with the job.

Beyond these informal and often unobtrusive processes lie the more formal ones of curriculum or course development, staff development (which may be related to appraisal) and organization development. The need for these seems so patent that it is difficult to see how problems can arise, but they do. The most common one is probably that everyone is so busy coping with immediate pressures and demands that there is simply no time or energy to invest in the longer-term development of staff, courses or the organization. Funds may be tight and those that are available may go to the wrong people or the wrong initiatives. There may be no coherent development strategy, or certain types of staff (eg, part-timers) or activities (eg, traditional courses) may get little support. Staff development may be seen in purely individual terms rather than tied into the work of the department. Staff appraisal may not work well, either because it has no consequences and is therefore not taken seriously, or because of conflicts between appraisal, managerial and collegial roles. New courses may be introduced in a rush with only minimal briefing or preparation of the people teaching them. The organization may engage in repeated restructuring without considering whether the problem is a structural one at all.

WHAT'S THE PROBLEM?

EFFECT ON TEACHING?

As with some other sections in this chapter, a lot depends on your own position in the organization, and whether you are on the decision making or receiving end. It also depends on the diagnosis you have made, and whether you think the problems are basically financial, structural or to do with the culture of the institution. Individuals may play a negative or blocking role; for example, a backward-looking head of department can make it very difficult for staff to introduce new ideas or develop new skills. Peer groups can also put pressure on colleagues who want to change things, or put obstacles in the way of those who already have.

You may get some ideas from the following.

- Try to ensure that there is a distinct budget line, however small, for staff development so that such funds do not simply become absorbed under other headings, especially when things get tight.
- Make the discussion of curriculum development a standing item on the course committee agenda and make sure that it is not at the bottom. It might usefully be put next to evaluation (Section 30).
- Are there periodic meetings or 'away days' when staff can review what they have done and identify new areas of development? It is often better to hold these events outside the institution so that people can get away from it both physically and mentally.
- Are there sufficient times and places for informal staff contact, for example over coffee or at lunchtime? Paradoxically, the demand for efficiency can prove inefficient over the longer term because the lack of time for such contact has to be compensated with formal meetings, or (more likely) the institution begins to lose know-how and 'organizational memory'.
- Is there a small fund for backing innovative ideas and initiatives such as creating new materials, using new technology, introducing new methods? You may be able to tap external funding for these: while core funding in post-compulsory education is currently tight, there are more small pots of money around for specific purposes than there used to be.
- Invite outside speakers periodically to talk about developments elsewhere or enable staff to visit other places where there are interesting things going on. Ask them to brief colleagues on their return.
- Try to address the downside of development: the sense of anxiety or insecurity that some staff (including you) may feel, or the threat of 'de-skilling' implied by some changes. Do not pretend that it is all always positive. Talk the issues through.

The main implications of such ideas would seem to be in terms of cost, organization, staff and time; their impact on assessment and students is likely to be more indirect.

A

SOLUTIONS

33 IS STAFF MORALE GOOD?

NO ☐   ? ☐   YES ☐

It is as important to think about staff morale as about student motivation, which we looked at way back in Section 7. In both cases, knowledge, strategies, skills and techniques are pointless without the will to use them. Staff may still keep going even when their morale is low. They do so because the sheer regularity of the work carries them along and the organization keeps them in harness. They also stay with it because of their own professionalism, a word that sometimes means doing the job even when you do not want to! However, as noted earlier, the nature of teaching means that staff have a great deal of what organization theorists call 'discretion' in the way they do the work. Most teaching goes on behind closed doors and its 'compliance observability' is therefore low. Although 'performance management' has led to greater visibility and openness, it is still difficult for any head of department or organization to keep tabs on everything and everyone all the time. The teacher's view of and attitude to the job can therefore affect the fine detail of his or her work: the way he or she deals with a student's question in class or afterwards, the care taken in marking assignments, the turnaround time, and so on. More subtly still, it affects the thought and energy that go into trying to develop practice and improve the teaching–learning process, and 'going the extra mile'.

- Is there a high sickness/absence rate among staff?
- Is there a high turnover rate?
- Is it easy to recruit new staff?
- Are staff willing to undertake 'extras'?
- Is there much internal conflict among staff?
- What is the general atmosphere like in the staffroom?
- Has staff morale changed markedly in (say) the last two years?

Many of the factors that affect staff morale are general or national. Contracts and conditions of service reflect nationwide patterns and norms. Pay scales are in most cases determined nationally, although there is increasing institutional variation in the form of fast tracks, merit awards and bonuses of various kinds. Most of the 'paperwork' of teaching stems from official requirements. While the status of teachers depends partly on the type of institution and the nature of the intake, it is widely felt to have declined. The growth of accountability represents, to some teachers at least, a collapse of trust and dilution of professional autonomy. There are counter-vailing factors – the increased availability of technology, the greater opportunities for continuing professional development, the decline in autocracy and arbitrary power – but to judge from the public utterances of teachers and lecturers the balance sheet has been largely negative in the last decade.

That sense cannot be ignored, but there is probably little that individual teachers or small groups of staff can do about it. This section concentrates therefore on staff morale in terms of the institutional or departmental 'micro-climate'. Here the key problems are likely to relate to three main factors. The first is the leadership exercised or exerted by the head of section, subject or department. This will become the main focus of the next section (34) but it is also a major influence on staff morale. The second concerns the relationships among staff. We should not expect teaching to be a conflict-free zone. The fact that it involves values and beliefs, that there is often no single or right way of doing things, that it is intimately enmeshed in human relationships, means that conflict is inherent in it. Teachers argue, have been trained to argue, and often quite like arguing. The question is whether these conflicts are managed, not only by those in charge but everyone involved, so that they are productive rather than destructive. The third factor is the institutional climate. Here we have only to think about the environment we try to create for learners to see the parallels for staff. The working environment should be reason-ably orderly, safe, supportive, rewarding and fair. What is good for students is good for staff.

There is one final point that, although it reflects national trends, can be addressed locally up to a point. One of the deepest and most disillusioning aspects of the current situation is the feeling many staff seem to have that they cannot get on with the job: that they cannot do what they came into the profession for. Various things may prevent them 'teaching' as they see it: behaviour and discipline problems, lack of external support, excessive emphasis on testing, poor equipment, increased bureaucracy and lack of continuity. Teachers come into teaching primarily because they want to or because it seems a reasonable choice in the circumstances, so the main factor affecting their morale is whether they are allowed to do the job. Are they? Are you?

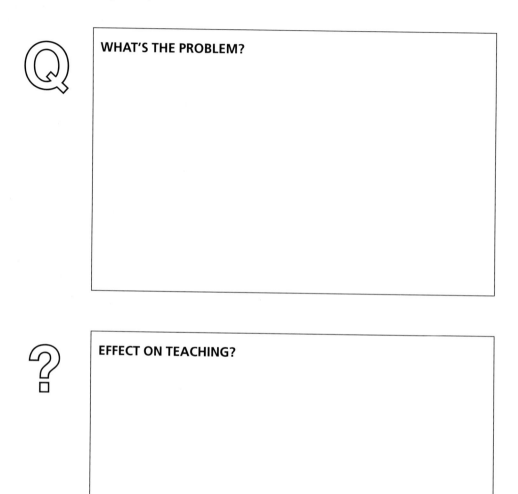

WHAT'S THE PROBLEM?

EFFECT ON TEACHING?

Here are some thoughts to be going on with.

- Praise where praise is due. As with students, one should not forget to say well done. And that applies not just to a head of department but to everyone, if collegiality is to be a reality.
- Staff can develop expertise in particular areas that interest them. On the whole, teaching is a generalist activity in the sense that it involves a wide range of skills (even if subject knowledge is specialized) and staff are expected to turn their hands to many things. However, allowing a degree of specialization may not only boost individuals' job satisfaction and sense of expertise but also lead to greater organizational efficiency.
- Do not neglect the social side of working together. Staff need times and places to meet and gossip. Not only does a lot of business get done informally in this way but such contact can provide mutual support. Otherwise, colleagues may simply not be aware of one another's problems.
- We seem to be in the grip of a rather grim work ethic at the moment. If there are successes, take time out to celebrate them. That will give everyone a lift and perhaps inspire others.
- Like students, staff sometimes work best not individually nor in large groups but in small clusters – three, four or five people who take in hand a particular task. This pattern allows the institution to tap a range of expertise and also guards against the sudden loss of knowledge or know-how when someone leaves. But it can also be quite enjoyable, avoiding both the loneliness of solo work and the lumbering progress of entire committees.
- Focus also on the pleasures of the work. What are they? What do staff – do you – enjoy about teaching? What rewards does it bring? Try to recognize and maximize these.
- If there is a major underlying conflict or problem that is having a serious effect on morale it has to be confronted. This is down primarily to the person in charge (see next section) but it also requires the support of other staff. If we believe that educational institutions are 'collegial' rather than purely 'hierarchical', we have to accept our part in making them work.

As well as the obvious implications for staff, this section has a bearing on the organization, and some solutions may involve additional costs.

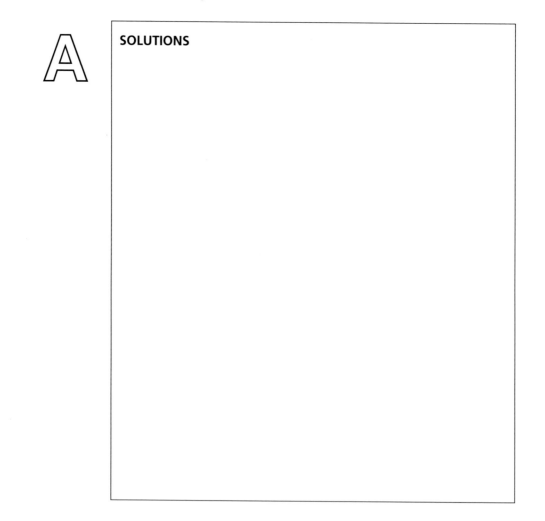

SOLUTIONS

34   IS THERE APPROPRIATE LEADERSHIP?

NO ☐   ? ☐   YES ☐

As has been pointed out several times, educational institutions are an odd mixture of the hierarchical and the collegial. There is a formal 'chain of command' but equally many decisions are taken or approved collectively by the staff. Thus when we talk about managing education, the question arises: Who are the managers? Are they those senior staff who have designated responsibilities for whole departments or even institutions, or is everyone to some degree responsible for managing his or her work? The same point applies to leadership. Does it reside mainly in an identifiable person or role, or is it a function that may be carried out by any number of people at various times or in one situation or another? Thus the question here is about leadership rather than leaders and is framed in relative terms: is there appropriate leadership in relation to teaching? Leadership is a composite concept, involving a range of possible attributes or functions; it may be more or less visible or necessary in different circumstances. So the answer to the question may vary from one time and place to another, and will, as with some of the other sections, depend on whether you are concerned with a particular unit, an entire department or the institution as a whole.

- Is there a leader?
- Is leadership concentrated or diffused through the organization?
- Is there enough leadership?
- Is there a clear sense of organizational priorities?
- Who takes the difficult decisions?
- Are there nettles that have not been grasped?
- Is there a shared vision?
- Is there a sense of drift?
- What about 'followership'? Do staff support the leader/leadership?

Leadership is an elusive concept. In the conventional imagination, it summons up the person who is out there directing operations, inspiring the rank and file, leading from the front. However, some people turn out with hindsight to have been very effective indirect leaders who somehow managed to work through their colleagues and get things done while still keeping a low profile themselves. And which sort of leadership anyway? Leadership about what? In what circumstances? How do leaders differ from managers, if indeed they do?

One way of getting at this slippery beast is negatively. When do we notice a lack of leadership? When do we complain that it is missing? One answer has to do with vision, that capacity to see where an organization should go in the future, to hold to one's objective through thick and thin and somehow to infuse and enthuse others with it. A second answer might relate to difficult choices, where eventually someone has to decide between several desirable courses of action. A variant of this might concern unpopular choices that have to override sectional interests, comfortable habits or short-termism. Leadership may also unify, helping a disparate organization to cohere, to hang together; this is often an important function in educational institutions that are naturally fissiparous. It can also play a critical role in the fire-fighting or crisis management described in Section 28. And leadership may simplify the inevitable complexity and multiplicity of everyday work by embodying an essential, steadying focus on a few key principles.

All of this can of course go wrong and become pathological or dysfunctional. Thus decisiveness may lead to autocracy, while the willingness to listen can degenerate into indecision. Interpersonal skills can lead to favouritism or the development of inner circles, negotiating skills become a matter of wheeling and dealing, a concern with presentation turns into mere spin. More often perhaps in education it is the sheer pressure of circumstances that erodes or undermines the leadership function, as those in charge simply have too many things to deal with to fulfil the broader roles listed above. There is also sometimes the problem that a member of staff who is good at something else – teaching, research – or has simply been around a long time gets promoted on that basis to a leadership position and turns out to be hopeless at it. All this brings us back to the idea of leadership as a quality that is somehow diffused and embedded among the staff, with different people taking the initiative at different times and in response to different challenges. However, that in turn implies a degree of devolution or delegation in the first place and a capacity for group decision making that may or may not exist.

WHAT'S THE PROBLEM?

EFFECT ON TEACHING?

As with some of the other management issues covered in this chapter, the potential solutions you come up with will depend very much on the kind of diagnosis you have made, and with a topic as elusive as leadership that can prove a difficult task in itself. Besides, different people view the whole notion of leadership in very different ways, depending partly on the hierarchical/collegial balance mentioned at the beginning, and on their own preferences for working in a relatively structured or unstructured environment. But here are some ideas that may in turn trigger others:

- The idea of 360° appraisal means that people are appraised not only by those above them but also those below and to the side. This might be worth considering.
- The need for leadership may sometimes be inversely related to the quality of organization: if everything runs smoothly there may be less need for someone to hold things together, make difficult decisions and so on. In thinking about leadership it is important therefore to ask the other questions about the department or institution that have been explored in Sections 27, 28, 29 and 30.
- Real change may sometimes require the new broom of a new head of institution, department or programme. Simply having a different person there seems to matter.
- Many of the points made about teachers as models (Section 18) also apply to the leadership of staff, and it is now generally recognized that 'modelling' in this sense can be a very important if not always conscious or overt aspect of leadership. Thus even if a head of department is not a particularly good administrator, he or she may provide a powerful model for staff. This aspect of leadership needs to be borne in mind in appointment decisions.
- Education is now much more closely linked to the external world than it used to be, and those with organizational or programme responsibilities need to be skilled in dealing with a wide range of external officials and stakeholders. Since teaching experience may not prepare one for this, it may require some additional training.
- Leadership typically involves a good deal of 'soft knowledge' about people, networks, relationships, conflicts, agendas and so on. Most of this is tacit rather than explicit, so it is important for potential leaders to have the opportunity to pick it up through mentoring, shadowing or other forms of 'cognitive apprenticeship'.
- Some of the most difficult leadership roles lie at the middle level of the organization (eg, head of department or section) where pressures from below meet demands from above, yet this can be the most critical level in terms of actually getting things done. It

is important to recognize the importance of this stratum and worth investing time and effort in preparing people for these jobs.

● Leadership responsibilities can be extremely demanding, so it may be wise to rotate or at least change the person in that role periodically. In some institutions, heads of department are given a sabbatical or some time off to recover afterwards.

● If you have a leadership role, you need to be available. It is no good if staff can never get to see you.

A

SOLUTIONS

The next, final section is on *resources*.

35 ARE THERE THE RESOURCES TO DO THE JOB?

NO ☐   ? ☐   YES ☐

This question has been deliberately left to the last. It is all too easy for teachers and lecturers to blame all their troubles on lack of resources, but before they do so they need to think whether they are making the best use of what they already have. So it was necessary to work through all the preceding sections in this chapter, to do with organization, planning, development, morale and so on before coming to this final crunch. The issue of resources came up before in Section 14 but there it was in the more limited sense of learning resources, that is, the materials that students need to pursue their learning. Here, 'resources' is being used in the generic sense of the financial, physical and human inputs to education. Some of these resources – sites, buildings, facilities, libraries, equipment – accumulate or depreciate over time, but most resources are more immediate or temporary than that, and this fact makes teaching particularly sensitive to short-term, year-on-year changes in funding. And, depending on the type of institution, 60–90 per cent of that funding may go on staffing. It is no wonder therefore that the most obvious indicators are those to do with human resources, such as funding/income per student, staff–student ratios or age profiles of staff. The question is a basic one: are there sufficient human and other resources to carry out the process of teaching effectively?

- What state are the buildings in?
- Are the staff and student facilities adequate?
- Is equipment up to date?
- Has the staff–student ratio increased or decreased over the last five years?
- Are there enough support staff of all kinds?
- How well does the system cope when under strain?
- Do staff generally feel fully employed or overworked? And how far is that perception or reality?

As pointed out above, raw measures of resources or inputs need to be interpreted in the light of how and how well they are used, and two institutions or programmes with the same level of funding can produce very different outputs from it. That said, the general level of funding matters for several reasons. First, it needs to be sufficient to maintain the infrastructure of teaching: the buildings, equipment, libraries, technology, materials and so on. Unfortunately, educational infrastructure can become run down over time without the effects becoming immediately apparent, and this allows governments and funding bodies to get away with inadequate upkeep for long periods of time until (metaphorically or otherwise) the roof falls in. Second, funding matters in terms of attracting and retaining good staff. Teaching for some people is a vocation. For others it is a 'reserve' occupation: something they go into because they cannot get into, or decide ultimately not to enter, other occupations. The package of rewards – both material and psychological – must be sufficient to attract the latter group as well as the former. That package includes working conditions (hours, holidays) and the working environment both in and outside the classroom, but a certain level of income is needed to recruit those whom the system and the profession need.

Funding also matters in terms of staff–student ratios. It should have become clear from the analysis in Chapters 1 and 2 that some functions of teaching are 'ratio-sensitive' while others are not. One can give orientation to or deliver an input to a class of any size. Likewise one may set tasks for 20 or 200 students. A well-designed and managed course is so for everyone, regardless of numbers. However, dovetailing new with prior learning, explaining things, dealing with problems, offering support or fostering self-belief, giving feedback or encouraging reflection require an individualized approach. So does most assessment. Such things simply take time, and the more time one has per student, the better one can do them. The more sophisticated, interactive forms of new technology go some way towards providing mass-but-individualized teaching, but the most subtle tasks go beyond even that.

Resource problems may be specific rather than general. There can be shortages of staff, materials or equipment in particular subjects or departments. In some cases, other staff will cover or fill in, but in the long run this is unsatisfactory because of the specialized nature of much of the subject matter at the post-compulsory level. This underlines the fact that resources in teaching are a matter not simply of staff bodies but of expertise: having the people who possess the knowledge and skills to do the job. And as the section on development (32) implied, such expertise has to be continually updated and renewed, and this also costs money.

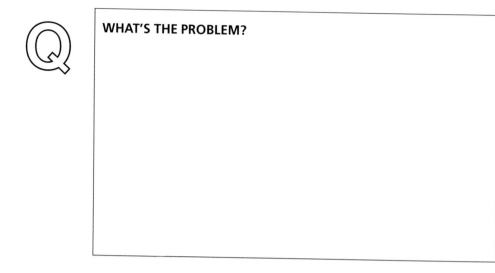

WHAT'S THE PROBLEM?

EFFECT ON TEACHING

Decisions about the general level of funding of teaching are taken nationally and are thus beyond your control, and your capacity to influence institutional or departmental decisions will depend on your own seniority and role. There may thus be sharp limits to the solutions you can propose in this final section but here are some possibilities:

- Beyond the general funding that its available, there are increasing numbers of specific projects or initiatives that attract funds, for example to do with new technology, widening participation or teaching quality. Do not miss out on these. It may be useful to have one member of staff look out for them and advise on which ones you can bid or apply for.
- Develop expertise in making bids for funds (this is particularly necessary if applying for EC funds, which can be a very complex process). Have a number of draft bids ready for when the right opportunity comes. The deadline for making applications is often quite tight.
- If some staff are overloaded, others may be under-used. Allow for some variations over time, but try to ensure that there is an equitable distribution of labour, perhaps through a workload model. However, such models need to be well designed if they are to command general assent.
- 'Flexible working' can lead to an erosion of professionalism and degradation of working conditions, but in other ways may open up new possibilities, as indeed it has in other occupations. Try to identify any serious rigidities in the system and find ways of overcoming them.
- Part-time staff often give more than they are paid for. That is not a licence to exploit them, but you should recognize that they can be a very valuable and committed resource. That means treating them well, not just as casual labour, and a real effort to involve them and recognize their contribution may be very welcome.
- Teachers' and lecturers' time seems to be increasingly taken up with things other than actually teaching (e-mails, paperwork, meetings). See if you can reduce these without prejudicing the accuracy of your records or quality of your procedures.
- If you work at a senior level, ensure that there is a running record of key staff indicators: ratio of applicants to advertised posts, age profiles, incremental drift, proportion of full-time and part-time, sickness rates, temporary replacements or supply teaching, turnover, staff–student ratios. This will allow you to monitor current trends and anticipate future problems.

Check your proposed solutions against the COSTAS headings.

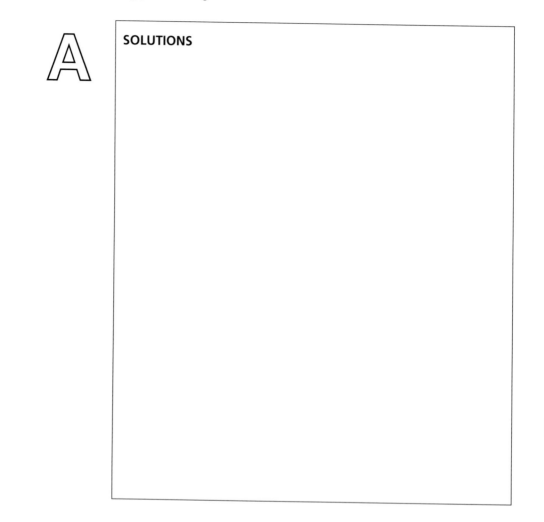

SOLUTIONS

Anything else?

Please add any other management issues that you think have not already
been covered in this chapter.

```
WHAT'S THE PROBLEM?



```

```
EFFECT ON TEACHING?



```

And, for the last time, remember COSTAS!

```
SOLUTIONS



```

Profile

Summarize your responses to the questions about 'Managing it all' on the table below by ringing the appropriate number. Remember that as you check back through each section, you will need to transpose your initial three-point judgement (NO / ? / YES) onto the seven-point scale as follows (NO = 1 or 2; ? = 3, 4 or 5; YES = 6 or 7). As before, reviewing the sections may lead you to alter your initial response in the light of subsequent work.

	No		?			Yes	
27. Are things well organized?	1	2	3	4	5	6	7
28. Are problems dealt with quickly?	1	2	3	4	5	6	7
29. Is there adequate planning?	1	2	3	4	5	6	7
30. Is there effective evaluation?	1	2	3	4	5	6	7
31. Is there sufficient stability?	1	2	3	4	5	6	7
32. Is there enough development?	1	2	3	4	5	6	7
33. Is staff morale good?	1	2	3	4	5	6	7
34. Is there appropriate leadership?	1	2	3	4	5	6	7
35. Are there the resources to do the job?	1	2	3	4	5	6	7
Anything else?	1	2	3	4	5	6	7

Please turn now to the final action plan opposite.

Action plan

As in the previous chapters, specify your aims, the various components or stages of the action, the person or persons responsible (which may be you) and the proposed time frame.

AIM	ACTION	PERSON	DEADLINE

What's going on?

The list of questions in Chapter 1 allows you to pinpoint certain aspects of your classroom teaching and to see whether they are working as well as you would wish. This is helpful in identifying and trying to deal with particular problems. However, if you want simply to explore your teaching and get a general picture of what is going on in a session, you can use the framework set out in this appendix. This activity is best done in pairs, so that you observe a colleague's teaching first and then your colleague observes yours. That allows you both to build up a mutual understanding of the process, and will almost certainly throw up contrasting issues, though you should eventually draw other people into the process as well so that it becomes a wider, collegial one. The person who is going to observe the class first needs to familiarize himself or herself with the framework, but it is not necessary to brief the teacher who is being observed. Indeed, it is better to let him or her proceed as normally as possible and to minimize any intrusion. The observer will need to be able to see and hear what is going on easily and record it on the form overleaf (a one-hour class may take several pages).

Let us assume that you are doing the observing. In the left-hand column note down the time about every five minutes. This will be useful afterwards in reconstructing the sequence of events, but need not be rigid. In the next column, note down briefly the topic or subject matter at that time. This will again help you and the teacher to reconstruct afterwards what went on in the class, and relate the analysis of teaching to the content. In the third column, try to record what function the teacher (and perhaps students) was performing at that time, as follows:

Functions

- *Audit:* identifying prior knowledge, skills or experience.
- *Orient:* establishing direction, objectives or agenda.
- *Input:* communicating or generating information (facts, ideas, practices).

Time	Topics	Functions	Variables	Activities	Comments

Table A.1 *What's going on?*

- *Explain:* clarifying, expanding or relating, checking understanding.
- *Task:* setting or supervising learning tasks or activities in or outside the class.
- *Feedback:* giving feedback to students on their work and progress.
- *Motivate:* stimulating interest or enthusiasm, challenging, inspiring.
- *Belief:* fostering self-confidence and self-efficacy, dealing with self-doubt.
- *Reward:* rewarding good work or effort individually or as a group.
- *Exploration:* developing open-ended, critical or creative thinking.
- *Reflection:* developing awareness of the learning process.

You may find that at some points the teacher is performing more than one of these functions and at other times appears to be doing none of them; for example, there might be some initial social chat or administrative paperwork to get through. Don't worry if you are sometimes unsure about the function; note down what you can for the moment so that you can discuss it with the teacher later. Remember that such functions may be fulfilled not only by the teacher but the students, so pay careful attention to what they are doing also, both for themselves and for one another.

In the next column (variables) try to record what is affecting or influencing the teaching at that moment. For example, the teacher may be responding to a particular student. S/he may be concerned with managing the group as a whole. S/he may be following a certain curriculum 'script' or trying to explain a particularly difficult point. Certain 'process' objectives – developing critical thinking, promoting teamwork – may be shaping what is going on. The nature of the room and facilities may create certain constraints or opportunities. There may be wider organizational or social factors coming into play. Don't worry if the entries in this column initially look a bit thin; many of them exist in the teacher's mind and will only come out when you talk to him or her afterwards. The key question is: what was affecting his/her teaching at this point? What was influencing or driving it? It might be any of the following:

Variables

- *Rationale:* the aims of the course or objectives of the session.
- *Content:* the nature of the subject matter or topic.
- *Process:* key, generic or transferable skills.
- *Level:* the level of the course or class.

- *Group:* the size, composition, dynamics and ethos of the group.
- *Individuals:* the characteristics of particular students.
- *Self:* the teacher's own personality, approach or style.
- *Physical setting:* the room, furniture, equipment, facilities.
- *Organizational setting:* the programme or departmental context.
- *Social setting:* the wider social and cultural context.

Obviously the influence of some of these will be more indirect or oblique than others and it can take time to tease out the extent to which someone's teaching is shaped or affected by them. For example, the social setting can impinge on teaching in all sorts of subtle ways, and the 'teacher-self' can be a sensitive area to explore. At some points in the class, there may seem to be one dominant variable (the nature of the topic, the reactions of the group), but often teaching involves a complex negotiation between variables and constitutes a kind of juggling act. (Should I respond to that student? If so, will I lose the rest of the group? Should I go into this in more detail? If so, will I run out of time? Have I said this already? Was that student there last week? Do I need to recap? And so on.)

In the next column, note down the methods or activities that were going on at that time. Remember to record not only what the teacher was doing but also the students' activities; if the teacher is talking, the students may be taking notes; if the teacher is asking questions, the students will be answering; if the teacher is helping one student, the others may be getting on with their work. The following is a standard list of classroom methods and activities but you may come across others:

Activities

- *Presentation:* lecture, talk, briefing.
- *Demonstration:* performance.
- *Question and answer:* exchange or dialogue.
- *Discussion:* interaction.
- *Simulation:* role play or game.
- *Practical:* exercise, experiment or activity.
- *Supervision:* tutoring or coaching.
- *Assignment:* homework or essay.
- *Project:* long essay or report.
- *Placement:* apprenticeship or shadowing.

Some of these activities take place outside the classroom itself, but it is important to include them if they form part of the total package of teaching. What goes on in the classroom should always be seen in the context of any prior or follow-up work. For example, if students have not done the preparatory reading, the teacher may have to give a talk instead of chairing a discussion; likewise, the students' attitude to the class may be shaped by the assignments they have to do or the exam they are preparing for. Some classes will consist of a bundle of methods and activities (initial talk followed by question and answer followed by practical task followed by general discussion followed by final talk), whereas others will consist of a single 'method' such as a lecture, seminar, laboratory session, workshop or individual supervision.

Finally, in the right-hand column note down any comments that come into your head at the time. These may relate to any of the functions, variables or activities and provide a useful *aide-memoire* for you. Some of them may be questions that you want to put to the teacher afterwards. Often a word or phrase will be enough to remind you.

As soon as possible after the class, and not more than a day later, explain what you were doing to the teacher and show him or her your notes. Talk through each stage in the session in terms of what function he or she was performing at that point, what was driving or affecting the teaching at that moment (subject? students? setting?) and what methods were being used. It can often take an hour or more to work through one session in this way. Remember that the point of the exercise is to 'unpack' the process rather than to evaluate it; your aim should be to help your colleague become more aware of what's going on, not to pass judgement on it. Ideally, you should repeat the exercise two or three times; each class throws up different issues and as the teacher begins to get the hang of the framework (which can seem quite complex at first) he or she will be in a better position to use and indeed question it. Remember also that no framework such as this can capture the full reality of teaching. Use it as a tool; don't be used by it.If you want to integrate this kind of exercise into an ongoing analysis of your teaching try keeping a teaching journal or diary that begins before such observations, continues during them and goes on afterwards for a while. By making an entry (say) twice a week you will develop a running commentary on your work in which any effects of the observation process may be picked up.

Whose job is it anyway?

One of the questions that has run through this book, and in particular Chapter 1, concerns the relative roles and responsibilities of students and teachers in the teaching–learning process. You can explore this with staff and/or students by taking the list of functions set out in the previous appendix and asking both groups to what extent they think it is their or the other's responsibility, using Figure A2.1.

	Student					Teacher	
			Audit				
X	X	X	X	X	X	X
			Orient				
X	X	X	X	X	X	X
			Input				
X	X	X	X	X	X	X
			Explain				
X	X	X	X	X	X	X
			Task				
X	X	X	X	X	X	X
			Feedback				
X	X	X	X	X	X	X
			Motivate				
X	X	X	X	X	X	X
			Belief				
X	X	X	X	X	X	X
			Reward				
X	X	X	X	X	X	X
			Explore				
X	X	X	X	X	X	X
			Reflect				
X	X	X	X	X	X	X

Figure A2.1 *Whose job is it anyway?*

Explain each heading and, as you do so, ask participants to draw a short vertical line somewhere on each spectrum to indicate the perceived locus of responsibility (ie, towards the left-hand end for the student, towards the right-hand end for the teacher). Then ask them to compare their responses and discuss the extent to which they agree or differ. You can get an instant group response by giving each subgroup an acetate and marker pen, asking them to collate (not average) the responses, and then superimposing all the acetates on an overhead projector (a bit messy but it works). Responses may converge or diverge. If the former, explore the basis of the consensus; if the latter, explore the reasons for the differences. For example, you might find that some people expect input to come mainly from the teacher, while others think that students should find such information or materials for themselves. Some people may believe that students should be self-motivating, while others will see more of a motivational role for the teacher. Some may regard reflection as largely a private matter for the student, others will regard it as something the teacher should encourage in the class. Differences can open up on any of the headings, though there is usually a consensus that feedback has to come mainly from the teacher. (But is this desirable? See Section 6.)

Discussion also tends to throw up an interesting range of variables. Some people will object (reasonably enough) that the position on each spectrum 'depends'. The locus of responsibility may be thought to be a matter of individual differences between students, the ethos of the group, the nature of the subject matter, the level of study, the stage in the course, the teacher's style, the assessment system, institutional norms, cultural expectations. . . all of which usefully illuminate the range of variables of teaching and learning listed in the previous appendix. There is thus no standard or simple answer to these questions, and this is an important point to make. You may also find differences between staff and student perceptions that can be explored and perhaps form the basis for working out a viable 'contract' as to who does what. The purpose of the exercise is thus not to promote a particular view of teaching and learning but to make both staff and students more aware of their expectations.

Guidelines for workshop leaders

You can use your own judgement and common sense in the way you employ this book in workshops or other structured staff development activities, but the following notes may be useful. There are two general points to bear in mind. First, the content of the workshop will depend on the role and position staff occupy in the institution, and this will suggest which chapter or chapters to use with them (perhaps refer back to Figure 0.1). Second, you should provide enough structure but not too much; the success of the workshop will depend on how well participants can use the framework that the book provides to come up with their own examples, diagnoses and solutions. Avoid too much presentation/input; leave plenty of time for group work. There are a number of more specific points:

- There is a lot in the book. Do not try to cover too much at one go; allow ample time for staff to contribute their own views and perspectives. A chapter can easily occupy half a day, and it is better and more satisfying to do a little in depth than a lot superficially.
- Apart from asking people to think about their teaching problems/concerns in advance, it is probably best to have them come fresh to the workshop, without doing any prior reading. If you do want them to prepare beforehand, they can work through a few sections on their own (eg, 1–6).
- You can ask participants to begin by working individually through the diagnostic parts of each chapter, then collate their profiles and see what pattern (if any) emerges. Participants can then work in small groups on possible solutions, with a plenary for everyone to report back.
- Try to build some 'thinking time' into the process, either within or (ideally) between workshops.
- Certain sections (eg, on intake, assessment and evaluation) may be more topical at certain times of year, and meet immediate needs.

- You can mix staff from different departments and levels, and this usually generates interesting contrasts as long as the divergences are not too great.
- Be prepared for the exercise to throw up criticisms of colleagues, management and the institution (not to mention the opportunity for a good moan about the world). Establish some ground rules for dealing with these.
- You can organize a follow-up workshop some months later to see what progress has been made on action plans.
- If you can offer some institutional support/funding for some actions, this will help give point to the whole exercise, and ensure that it is not seen simply as a talking-shop.
- As noted in the first appendix ('What's going on?') these kinds of activities can be usefully combined with longer-term teaching diaries, so that the experience feeds into continuing reflection on practice.

4 A note for foreign readers

While this book is about teaching in general, there are occasional references to the English system on which it is based. The following note explains the relevant terms.

Compulsory education ends at the age of 16 by which time pupils will usually have gained a number of GCSEs (General Certificate of Secondary Education). This is a single subject rather than grouped qualification and the level of attainment ranges from no or a few subjects to ten or more; 5 GCSEs at Grade C or above is often used as a national benchmark. Although most GCSEs are in traditional school subjects, some are more vocationally inclined and pupils can opt to take some vocational qualifications as well or instead.

Beyond this point the system exhibits the tripartite academic/technical/vocational structure which one finds in many industrialized countries (see Squires, G (1989) *Pathways for Learning: Education and training from 16 to 19*. Paris: OECD; also published in French as *Les Adolescents à la Croisee des Chemins*.) Students on the academic track typically study for two or three A levels (Advanced Level) taken at about the age of 18 which may be preceded or complemented by some AS levels (Advanced Supplementary Level) which are equivalent to half an A level and normally taken a year earlier. They can do this by staying on in the upper secondary school 'sixth form' (if there is one) or moving to a sixth form, tertiary or further education college, all of which provide for the 16–19 age group. However, the main work of the last is providing technical and vocational courses for both young people and adults, though FE colleges also cater for a wide range of community needs, including those of under-achieving or disadvantaged students. Technical courses, such as those leading to a Business and Technician Education Council award (BTEC/EDEXCEL) or a General National Vocational Qualification (GNVQ) most of which have recently been re-designed and re-designated as Vocational A levels, tend to be full time, relatively broad and have an applied theoretical basis. They often provide a 'second route' into higher education. Vocational courses, typically leading to an NVQ (National Vocational Qualification) and examined by bodies such as the City and Guilds of London Institute (CGLI), Royal Society of Arts (RSA) or London Chamber of Commerce (LCC) are more specific and practical. Both technical and vocational courses are subsumed within a national framework of vocational qualifications, although there are a number of different and relatively independent examining bodies. There are also apprenticeship schemes in some occupational sectors, but these are by no means as extensive or well established as in some continental European countries.

Access to higher education (HE) is by the direct A level route or indirect technical routes, with special access courses and requirements for adult 'mature students'. Degree courses are relatively short (three or four years) and specialized by international standards and often organized on a modular-credit basis, with a common currency of 120 credits per year at three undergraduate levels (Certificate, Intermediate and Honours). There has also been a growing emphasis on key, transferable skills initially in FE and now in HE as well.

Adult students may attend FE or HE institutions on a full-time but more usually part-time basis, but there are also adult education services run by municipalities and counties. Such courses range from adult basic education (comprising literacy, numeracy and basic skills) through non-assessed non-vocational education (related to personal, home and leisure interests to general or vocational qualifications, including GCSEs.

There have been two main trends in recent education policies. The first has been to introduce greater differentiation of both institutions and curricula within the compulsory, secondary system, with 14+ being increasingly regarded as a curricular watershed. The other has been to facilitate access and progression across the whole post-compulsory field and this has meant some blurring of the institutional and curricular boundaries described above. Another characteristic of educational policy in recent decades has been the tendency to introduce a large number of initiatives or discrete measures which do not always add up to coherent planning. The above pattern exists, with some minor variations, in England, Wales and Northern Ireland; the Scottish system has always been, and remains, different.

Further reading

This final section summarizes the theoretical basis for the book and lists those publications where it is set out in detail, so that you can explore it further if you wish to. These publications themselves contain extensive references that relate to most of the topics covered in the book, and provide the foundation for what is said here. However, some additional sources on specific points are also given below.

What do they do? What affects what they do? And how do they do it? These three questions form a useful framework for thinking about any profession. Here, they are applied to teaching and its management. The three questions stem originally from Aristotle's concept of *poiesis* and in particular his account of medicine (see Squires, G (in press) '*Praxis:* a dissenting note', *Journal of Curriculum Studies*). Although Aristotle was the first to draw the distinction between theory and practice, the way he employed these terms was very different from the way we typically use them today. They were formulated in the context of a wider discussion on the nature of the good life and related primarily to aspects or walks of life: *theoria* referred to the philosophical life with its connotations of contemplation, detachment and understanding, whereas *praxis* referred to the conduct of public and private life. Aristotle did not talk about the relationship (or gap) between theory and practice because for him they were two quite different domains, each with its own kind of thinking.

Occupations and specific activities fell under a third and less familiar heading, *poeisis*. This is sometimes translated as 'making', but the real sense is of an activity that aims to produce something beyond itself: some artefact or effect. All but the simplest forms of *poiesis* constitute a *techne*, and Aristotle gives over thirty examples of *technai*, ranging from manual crafts through sports and arts to activities that in our day we would regard as professions: architecture, military leadership, and in particular medicine, which he refers to frequently (his father was a physician).

There are three things that all these different activities have in common. They are functional in the sense of being directed towards and leading to some kind of outcome, and thus have to be judged in terms of that. Second, they are contingent or variable, in the sense of dealing with things that are changeable rather than immutable, and thus always have to be situated or placed in context. Third, they all involve ways and means – techniques, methods, procedures, processes – of doing what they do. Hence the three questions with which we began.

By putting these three questions together we can create a three-dimensional model of teaching, management or other professions (see Squires, G (1999) *Teaching as a Professional Discipline*, London: RoutledgeFalmer; Squires, G (2001) 'Management as a professional discipline', *Journal of Management Studies*, **38** (4), pp 473–487; Squires, G (2002) 'Modelling medicine', *Medical Education*, **36**, pp 1–6). Chapters 1 and 2 are underpinned by models of teaching and course provision, and Chapter 3 by a model of management. Such models offer a broad framework for analysing the activity, but they are not prescriptive; they suggest what we should think about or take account of, but they do not tell us precisely what to do. This book thus offers a general structure for thinking about teaching, and lists some possible solutions to problems, but only you are in a position to choose the best course of action in the light of your own particular situation.

The sections in each chapter correspond broadly to the 'functions' identified in each of the three models, though with some changes. The 'variables' and 'means' then emerge in the analysis of problems and discussion of solutions. However, the main difference between this and many other books on teaching is that it is organized around functions rather than methods or procedures. Teaching is not methods, it is what we do with methods. As has been emphasized many times in the text, the functions of teaching may well be shared not only among colleagues but between teacher and student. In that sense, it is equally a book about learning.

Notes

The following notes relate to points that are not covered in the references in the publications listed above. Since this is intended to be a mainly practical book, they have been kept to a minimum and restricted where possible to a few general sources.

Page

11   See Squires, G (1999) *Teaching as a Professional Discipline*, RoutledgeFalmer, London, pp 75–93.

12   The point was made many years ago by Robert Gagne in *The Conditions of Learning* (1969), Holt, Rinehart and Winston, London, pp 59–61. For a more recent discussion of different types of learning, see Jarvis, P, Holford, J and Griffin, C (2001) *The Theory and Practice of Learning*, Kogan Page, London.

18   Most general textbooks on educational psychology have something on the Pygmalion effect or teacher expectations; see for example Biehler, R F and Snowman, J (1993) *Psychology Applied to Teaching*, 7th edn, Houghton Mifflin, Boston, pp 568–72, or Child, D (1997) *Psychology and the Teacher*, 6th edn, Continuum, London, pp 71–72.

20   The specific reference here is to some previous research by the author: Gear, J, McIntosh, A and Squires, G (1994) *Informal Learning in the Professions: Final research report*, University of Hull Institute for Learning, Hull.

21   The best known is also one of the oldest: Bloom, B S *et al* (1956) *Taxonomy of Educational Objectives*, Longman, London.

21   There is a detailed discussion of the hidden curriculum in Meighan, R and Siraj-Blatchford, I (2000) *A Sociology of Educating*, 3rd edn, Continuum, London.

22   The formulation of key, generic or transferable skills varies from one sector to another, so you will need to consult the relevant literature for sixth forms, further education, or higher education. However, a useful general book is Assiter, A (ed) (1995) *Transferable Skills*

in Higher Education, Kogan Page, London. On the underlying psychological issues in the transfer of learning, see Biehler, R F and Snowman, J (1993) *Psychology Applied to Teaching*, 7th edn, Houghton Mifflin, Boston, pp 460–465.

23   The concept of advance organizers was first formulated by the American psychologist David Ausubel in the 1960s; see any of his books.

26   For an account of theories of learning see a general textbook such as Biehler, R F and Snowman, J (1993) *Psychology Applied to Teaching*, 7th edn, Houghton Mifflin, Boston; Child, D (1997) *Psychology and the Teacher*, 6th edn, Continuum, London; or Fontana, D (1995) *Psychology for Teachers*, 3rd edn, Macmillan/British Psychological Society, London.

31   The deep–surface distinction was originally formulated by the Swedish researcher Ferens Marton and has generated a good deal of subsequent research, mainly in higher education. For a recent discussion, see Prosser, M and Trigwell, K (1999) *Understanding Teaching and Learning: The experience in higher education*, Open University Press/Society for Research into Higher Education, Buckingham.

33   See Bloom, B S *et al* (1956) *Taxonomy of Educational Objectives*, Longman, London.

45   For a general account of theories of motivation see Biehler, R F and Snowman, J (1993) *Psychology Applied to Teaching*, 7th edn, Houghton Mifflin, Boston; Child, D (1997) *Psychology and the Teacher*, 6th edn, Continuum, London; Fontana, D (1995) *Psychology for Teachers*, 3rd edn, Macmillan/British Psychological Society, London; or Dornyei, Z (2001) *Teaching and Researching Motivation*, Longman, London.

49   See Goleman, D (1998) *Working with Emotional Intelligence*, Bloomsbury, London.

50   For an introduction to attribution theory, see Hayes, N and Orrell, S (1998) *Psychology: An introduction*, 3rd edn, Longman, London, pp 324–328.

53   See any of the general textbooks on educational psychology referred to above.

62   See Chapter 5 on 'Theory, expertise and practice' in Squires, G (1999) *Teaching as a Professional Discipline*, RoutledgeFalmer, London, pp 109–139.

63   See Squires, G (2002) *Managing Your Learning*, Routledge, London.

88   See Chapter 3 on 'Analyzing this course' in Squires, G (1999) *Teaching as a Professional Discipline*, RoutledgeFalmer, London, pp 37–74.

99   The origins of social learning theory and the concept of modelling are set out in Bandura, A (1986) *Social Foundations of Thought and Action*, Prentice-Hall, Englewood Cliffs, NJ. There are brief introductions in Biehler, R F and Snowman, J (1993) *Psychology Applied to Teaching*, 7th edn, Houghton Mifflin, Boston, and Jarvis, P, Holford, J and Griffin, C (2001) *The Theory and Practice of Learning*, Kogan Page, London.

100 See the second volume of Bloom on the affective domain: Krathwohl, D R *et al* (1964) *Taxonomy of Educational Objectives*, Longman, London.

109 There is now a large literature on informal adult learning; see for example Candy, P (1991) *Self-Direction for Lifelong Learning*, Jossey-Bass, San Francisco, or Tennant, M (1997) *Psychology and Adult Learning*, 2nd edn, Routledge, London.

124 For some practical ideas see Chapter 5 in Race, P (ed) (2001) *2000 Tips for Lecturers*, Kogan Page, London.

137 See Squires, G (2001) Management as a professional discipline, *Journal of Management Studies*, **38** (4), pp 473–487.

137 For a classic critique of rational planning see Lindblom, C (1959) The science of 'muddling through', *Public Administration Review*, **19** (2), pp 79–88.

140 See Becher, T and Trowler, P (2001) *Academic Tribes and Territories: Intellectual enquiry and the cultures of disciplines,* 2nd edn, Open University Press/Society for Research into Higher Education, Buckingham.

144 Beckett, D (1996) Critical judgement and professional practice, *Educational Theory*, **46** (2), pp 135–149.

148 See Lindblom, C (1959) The science of 'muddling through', *Public Administration Review*, **19** (2), pp 79–88; and Lindblom, C (1979) 'Still muddling, not yet through', *Public Administration Review*, **39** (6), pp 517–526.

157 These and other training issues are covered in Patrick, J (1992) *Training: Research and Practice*, Academic Press, London and Buckley, R and Caple, J (2000) *The Theory and Practice of Training*, 4th edn, Kogan Page, London.